Historical Perspectives on Dance in Africa

Historical Perspectives on Dance in Africa

Ofosuwa M. Abiola

INTELLIGENTSIA PRESS
Temple Hills

Intelligentsia Press
4806 Saint Barnabas Road, #493
Temple Hills, MD 20757

Intelligentsia Press is an imprint of Djole Arts Association, Inc.
www.djolearts.org/intelligentsia

© 2020 Ofosuwa M. Abiola
All rights reserved. No part of this book may be reprinted or reproduced or utilized in any form or by any electronic, mechanical, or other means, now known or hereafter invented, including photocopying and recording, or in any information storage or retrieval system, without permission in writing from the publisher.

Figures and tables with no attribution indicated are in the public domain.

Library of Congress Cataloguing-in-Publication Data
A catalogue record for this book has been requested.

Paperback ISBN: 978-1-7333571-0-4

Cover design by Araaku A.

Front cover photograph by Manojiit Tamen

For the Creator

For the preservation
of African dance history

Contents

List of Illustrations ix
Preface xi

1 Introduction 3

2 A Little History and Theory Goes A Long Way 7
What is Culture? 7
Geography, Climate & Culture in Africa 11

3 Southern Africa 21
The !Kung Healing Dance 26
Nyanga Flute Dance 32

4 Northern Africa 37
Egyptian Dance from Nubian Culture 37
The Gnawa: History, Culture and Dance 44

5 Eastern Africa 55
Ethiopia's National Dance 60
Burundi: History and the Arrival of the Tutsi 63

6 Western Africa 71
Kasa, Dance of the Ajamat 75
Yoleli and the Fulani 81

7 Central Africa 87

Chad, Mbaye, and the Klag 90
The Mwaash Mbooy: A Bushong Royal Dance 95

8 Conclusion 99

Appendix I. Table of African Dances 101
About the Author 109
Bibliography 111
Index 119

Illustrations

Figures

2.1	Low Torso	10
2.2	Medium Torso	10
2.3	High Torso	10
3.1	!Kung Healing Dance	27
3.2	!Kung Healer	27
3.3	San Dance Ritual	29
3.4	San Healing Dance	29
3.5	Ritual Nyanga Dance	33
3.6	Playing Nyanga	33
4.1	Two Pairs of Muu Dancers	42
4.2	A Pair of Muu Dancers	42
4.3	Gnawa at Marrakesh Market	48
4.4	Gnawa Dancer Leaping	52
5.1	Rock Church at Lalibela	60
5.2	Eskista Performance	62
5.3	Intore Dance of Heroes	68
6.1	Kasa, Corichow Dance Troupe	77
6.2	Gambian National Dance and Music Troupe	77
6.3	Kutiro Drum	78
6.4	Fulani Dancer	82
7.1	Kiantapo Cave Engravings	89
7.2	Mbaye Orchestra	92
7.3	Mwaash Mbooy Masked Dancer	96

Maps

2.1 Political Map of Africa	12
2.2 Africa's Terrain	14
3.1 Southern Africa	22
3.2 Mozambique	31
4.1 Northern Africa	38
4.2 Political Map of Morocco	45
4.3 Morocco and Western Sudan	45
5.1 Eastern Africa	56
5.2 Map of Ethiopia	52
5.3 Contemporary Map of Burundi	64
6.1 Map of Western Africa	72
6.2 The Gambia	74
7.1 Central Africa	88
7.2 Democratic Republic of the Congo	94

Tables

2.1 Rivers and Bodies of Water in Africa	16

Preface

The plight of the historian determined to create accounts that largely dispenses with the stronghold political history narratives have on academia is not a light one. My scholarly journey is further challenged by the fact that I believe that a true understanding of culture cannot be reached without a thorough survey of the history of the culture in question. Culture is not static. It is volatile. It is acted upon and influences life in general and lifestyles specifically. Anything that comes from culture, such as dance, must take all this into account. All my dance history books, therefore, include a large portion on the history of the culture under study. How can they not? For example, the environmental history of a region dictates what kinds of materials the people in any given culture of that region have available for the construction of ritual masks, textiles, props, and so on. It determines what people eat and how they will negotiate – through dance and other cultural phenomena – with the environment and the cosmos to assure that the food supply continues. The history of the environment also can reveal the types of aliments that befall its people, and the corresponding healing dances and other devices that will alleviate such. Thus, environmental history provides valuable insights into the culture of the people, and to reiterate, dance comes from and is part and parcel of the culture. African dance history is under-researched to say the least. Thus, environmental history research can reveal pieces of the dance portion of a cultural puzzle plagued with blank spots.

Knowledge of the history of the culture and ethnic groups responsible for creating that culture can fill in the other gaps in the narrative. Consequently, African dance history books that I write contain large concentrations of history – cultural, social, and environmental specifically. This is not to say that I will not also include political history accounts, but the emphasis will always be on the cultural decisions, aspirations, and behaviors of the actors in the African dance history narratives I write.

My methodology must be discussed at this juncture because it is common knowledge among historians that our field is founded upon the interrogation of written documents – the more ancient, the more credible. This fact could be potentially problematic for the African dance history scholar because written documents in Africa are seemingly not as abundant as in other areas such as Europe, and possibly the Middle East. Some scholars have even split the world into two categories, oral and writing cultures, wholly relegating the continent of Africa to the former.[1] The problem with this notion is writing *did* and does exist in Africa. From the millennia-old pictographs depicted on South African rock art, and ancient Egyptian writing, to the Ethiopian script Ge'ez, the Ghanaian Adinkra symbols, Nigerian Ikom inscriptions, and the Nubian Meroe scripts yet to be deciphered, among others, writing was no stranger to Africa. Nonetheless, the African vehicle of choice for documenting culture is culture itself. Subsequently, historians cannot apply the same methodologies for constructing historical accounts in Africa as they do for European historical research. Historical events, new developments in cultural phenomena, and age-old constants are housed, preserved, and revealed through the

---

[1] See Phillip B. Zarrilli et al., eds., *Theatre Histories: An Introduction*, 2nd ed (New York: Routledge, 2006).

culture generally, and dance specifically in Africa. Yet, an analysis of traditional dances in Africa requires foundational knowledge of the culture, and the ability to communicate with the practitioners of the dances – all of which can be obtained via oral history.

Although shunned by many orthodox historians, oral history is a viable methodology for African dance historical inquiry. Only the dance practitioners can convey the personal and objective meaning behind the dances. They can expose constants at the core of the dances, can inform scholars of new developments, and the information they provide can facilitate a more nuanced understanding of the historical events that surround, influence, and are impacted on by the dance systems being studied. Thus, it would have been impossible to write this book without utilizing oral history as one of my methodologies.

Last, it is important to emphasize I wrote this book with undergraduate students with little or no prior knowledge of African history, culture, or African dance history in mind. My years of teaching undergraduate history courses revealed the reality that many college students know very little if anything about history in general. The history knowledge dearth is greater with regard to African history generally, and African cultural history particularly. Although this work was written to be a textbook, my goal is to make the information in this book accessible to everyone. Since accessibility was the driving force, where possible, in addition to my own pictures I took on my various trips to Africa, I include many photographs that are readily available online in the public domain.

Ofosuwa M. Abiola, 2019

1 Introduction

Dance is More

Dance is more than the execution of patterned or rhythmic movements of a body. Dance is a lens that reveals the worldview, identity, and aspirations of peoples of ancient and contemporary societies. It is a primary source for the construction of historical accounts because it is derived from the people and cultures under study. Dance communicates ideas, feelings, traditions, and methodologies universally without the limitations posed by language. Dance documents and preserves historical accounts and showcases current developments in society.

Additionally, African dance is complex and must be approached as a dance *system* to obtain access to the rich information embedded within it. Thus, the dance movements and the dancer, the attire, the props used while performing the dance, the location where the dance is performed, the time of the year and month, the drummers and other musicians and their attire, the interactions between the dancers and drummers, and the songs sung before, during, and after the dance, are components of the dance system. All these elements facilitate comprehension and confirmation of the message conveyed by the dance. Moreover, greater appreciation of the dance system is obtained when foundational knowledge of the larger culture that gave birth to the dance system is examined.

Issues with Common Notions of Dance

Dance is omitted from scholarly conversations in the field of history. Any survey of books in bookstores and online that include academic and trade books, exposes the reality that historical narratives on anything other than political history are overwhelmingly omitted or under-represented. Retail and online history book collections are replete with titles discussing World War II, the Civil War, or the rise and fall of governments, presidents or other heads of states. A few titles focusing on social history and perhaps a rare title on cultural history may be found in an obscure corner on a shelf in a bookstore or unexpectedly included in a digital catalog, but for the most part, books on these subjects are grossly under-represented.

In unconventional historical circles, books on the history of dance are also generally not included. They may be found in specialty stores or set-aside categories in digital collections, but for the most part, dance history is relegated to the exotic, solely entertainment, or the obscure. This grim scenario is exponentially increased for African dance and its history.

African dance is not considered a viable scholarly topic of inquiry by society or academia outside of anthropology. It is restricted to notions of existing as a "tribal" and "raw" relic as opposed to a refined, complex, or sophisticated artform. Those who practice African dance are not expected to be poised and graceful only "earthy" or explosive. While fiery dance expressions have their place in African dance – as they do in many other styles of dance – there are also African dances that are performed gracefully and are replete with historical narratives. Additionally, and contrary to popular belief, dynamic or percussive dance movement does not preclude grace. Fallacies such as this can be alleviated through research. However, scholarly studies on African dance are routinely not conducted by historians, humanists and social scientists. Thus, the rich narratives in African dance systems are largely undiscussed.

Much can be learned about the history of a culture, a people, or a polity from African dance systems by studying them in their natural state, examining their development, and their present manifestations. Moreover, although currently not often discussed in scholarly literature, an African ballet format exists. This format facilitates the display of traditional African dance on the concert stage. More important, the African dance ballet format allows for contemporary issues to be discussed through dance narratives. Les Ballets Africains, the preeminent dance company founded by Guinean national, Keita Fodeba, has performed ballets on issues such as Female Genital Mutilation (FGM), the importance of retaining tradition in the midst of globalization, and the need to fight injustice, among other things.[2] These ballets would have exposed scholars to valuable information about African culture, history, the African mindset past and present, and life in general.

---

[2] Keita Fodeba was a Guinean national and the founder of Les Ballets Africains (LBA). He founded LBA in 1952 during the colonial period while he was studying in France. When his native country, Guinea, achieved independence in 1958, the new head of state, Sekou Toure, invited Fodeba to return with the company. Toure then nationalized the dance company. It became Les Ballets Africains de Guinea, and the first government supported African dance company in post-independent Africa. For extensive discussion on the founding of Les Ballets Africains, see Ofosuwa M. Abiola, *History Dances: Chronicling the History of Traditional Mandinka Dance* (London: Routledge, 2019), 129-32. See Le Ballet Africains, The National Dance Company of the Republic of Guinea. *Jubilee*. DVD. World Music Productions, Inc., 2004; and Le Ballet Africains, The National Dance Company of the Republic of Guinea. *Memoire du Manding*. DVD. Large Scale Productions, LLC and World Arts Inc., 2007.

2 A Little History & Theory Goes A Long Way

What is Culture?

Definitions of culture vary by the field or discipline. For the purposes of this study, culture is defined as the arts, intellectual and other achievements, customs, religious and social institutions of a particular nation, people, or social group. It is passed through the generations, and it is both static and dynamic. Culture includes dance, music, religion, language, food acquisition, choices, and eating habits, attire and so on.

Human life began on the continent of Africa and subsequently, it is also the birthplace of human culture. Thus, the continent of Africa is significant to all cultures. For example, language began in Africa before humans migrated to diverse locations on earth.[3] As they adapted to their new environments, their language was altered to accommodate their new experiences and terrains. Regardless of the alterations, all languages were based on the linguistic foundations developed in Africa and brought to other areas of the earth via migration.

Culture is learned. It is passed down through generations in families. Similarly, it is shared and continued throughout time in societies. Longevity notwithstanding, due to the infinite

---

[3] For a discussion on the African origin of language See, Quentin D. Atkinson, "Phonemic Diversity Supports A Serial Founder Effect Model of Language Expansion From Africa," *Science* 332, no. 6027 (April 15, 2011): 346-49, accessed July 3, 2019, https://doi.org/10.1126/science.1199295.

factors that dictate the structure and nature of cultural phenomena, some cultural tenets change, are discontinued, or are created.

Deconstructing the Word "Tribe"

The words "tribe" or "tribal" are often utilized when people from the West (Europe and America) refer to the activities of people of Africa and other non-Western peoples. Yet, when describing the same sort of activities engaged in by Westerners, the word "tribe" is virtually never employed. For example, traditional African dance is "tribal" dance, but traditional European dance is "folk dance." What would be referred to as a civil war in Europe or America is often called a tribal war in Africa. Truth be told, the word "tribe" is often accompanied by a value judgement. Whether one is conscious of it or not, tribe in the West usually denotes small bands of culturally or technologically backward people. It connotes a timeless state of developmentally arrested activities or people, savagery, and primitiveness.[4]

In this book, the word "tribe" will not be utilized. Instead, the terms ethnic group, nation, polity, and state, will be used to describe and discuss African people.

Dance Terms

Although the history of African dance is the focus of this book, at least a rudimentary knowledge of dance movement terms should be introduced to create a common frame of reference in

---

[4] For a discussion on the misleading use of the word "tribe" see, Christopher Ehret, *The Civilizations of Africa: A History to 1800* (Charlottesville: University of Virginia Press, 2016), 7.

the discussion that follows. Space does not permit an exhaustive discussion of dance terminology, though a few common dance terms will be helpful.

Movement vocabulary describes the specific types of body movements used by a dancer to express specific ideas or emotions. A step is a conglomeration of body movements. A *phrase* is a short section, usually of a larger choreographed dance piece, but it can exist by itself as well. A phrase can also be a sequence of steps performed together. Dance phrases typically contain more than one step or movement, and they have a beginning and an end. *Contractions* are executed by redundantly moving either the torso (the ribcage region) or the pelvic area (hip region) of the body forward and backward. The movement of the torso or the hips from side to side does not constitute a contraction. For example, the contemporary dance movement known as twerking is an example of pelvic contractions. A contemporary example of torso contractions are the torso movements heavily applied in the contemporary dance form krumping.

The torso is the part of the body located between the shoulders and the hips. It the ribcage and the entire mid-section of the body. Many traditional African dance movements employ an acute torso. That is, a torso that is at a less than ninety-degree angle to the ground. Three categories are recognized as acute torsos – low, medium, and high. When a low torso is executed it can be recognized by its appearance as almost parallel to the ground. The dancers' knees can be bent – which comes with its own set of categories – or straight. Dancers executing movements with high torsos appear to be dancing with nearly completely erect backs. Medium torsos are recognized as the positions in-between high (nearly erect) and low (parallel to the floor) torsos. Thus, there are several torso positions that can be characterized as a medium torso.

Figure 2.1 Low Torso Rite of passage ceremony, Zimbabwe, 2014.

Photograph: Terydanphiri

Figure 2.2 Medium Torso The Gambian National Dance and Music Troupe, USA, 1998.

Photograph: Chris Watson

Figure 2.3 High Torso Author in a high torso position, USA, 2007.

Photograph: Sidney Lily

Figures 2.1, 2.2, and 2.3 display the execution of high, medium, and low torsos. The torso positions are determined by the angle the torso – or back and ribcage – make with the floor. Hence, the term acute (as in less than ninety degrees) torso. Take note that the position of the knees – bent or straight – have no bearing on the torso position. Further, leaps can be executed with the torso in any position.

Although often utilized to assess visual art, the word *aesthetic* can facilitate a more comprehensive understanding of African dance systems. The term *aesthetic* is often used to describe how an item appears, and often refers to its beauty. However, for our purposes, the definition of aesthetic will not include a value judgement. It will be used to describe form only. For example, *aesthetic* will describe lines and angles of the body, apparent patterns, the appearance of movements that are witnessed only in specific regions of Africa or only in specific cultures, and so on. Last, *improvisation* is the act of performing unrehearsed, spontaneous dance movements or the creation of instantaneous inventive embellishments to dance steps. Now that we have a system for understanding general types of movement, dances from specific regions of Africa can be discussed in conjunction with the cultural history they emerged from.

Geography, Climate, and Culture in Africa

The geography and the climatic conditions in Africa are intimately linked and as a single phenomenon, they inform and facilitate culture. Consequently, Africa's diverse cultures are a reflection of the diverse terrains and climatic circumstances on the continent. In order to fully appreciate the dances, the cultures they are born of, the history, and people of Africa, a fundamental understanding of the geography and climate is warranted.

Africa is 11.67 million square miles. It is the second largest continent on earth. Its massive terrain can fit Europe, another continent, inside of it three times.[5] The age of the continent is also noteworthy. Over the course of billions of years, the climate has changed many times throughout the geological epochs and historical ages that characterized the continent. At one time in the continent's history, Africa was a component of Pangea, a supercontinent that existed 510-180 million years ago. Over millennia, the other continents separated from Pangea, were submerged in water, rose, split off, and so on. The nature of Africa's external landmass remained unchanged. However, myriad changes within the continent itself were witnessed.

---

[5] Many discussions on the size of Africa display a number of countries placed inside the continent of Africa for comparison. Such comparisons can be misleading. Since Africa is a continent, our discussion compares another continent, Europe, to Africa to illustrate Africa's enormous size.

12 A Little History & Theory Goes a Long Way

Map 2.1 Political Map of Africa

Map 2.1 displays the contemporary political map of Africa. Note that South Sudan, the newest country in Africa – it split from Northern Sudan in 2011 – is included. In the late nineteenth century, European countries colonized Africa and divided it according to their whims. The longstanding cultural and national boundaries in Africa were not considered. The colonial partition of Africa remained after independence. Thus, the current country boundaries are portrayed on the map solely for a frame of reference. Many of the cultures discussed in this study existed prior to the present borders.

While Europe experienced its Ice Age, Africa was undergoing a Dry Age (no ice). Deserts grew beyond what they are today. Lakes and streams shrunk or dried up completely. During wet phases, the opposite occurred, deserts decreased in land mass or disappeared. Between thirty thousand and ten thousand years ago, the Sahara was a wet region capable of supporting vegetation and wildlife. A band of lakes and swamps were stretched across the southern region of the Sahara. Lake Chad grew so large that it encompassed portions of what would become the modern-day countries of Nigeria, Cameroon, Niger, and Chad. Although small in size today, modern Lake Chad serves as a reminder of the ancient Mega-lake that once covered an area of over one hundred fifty thousand square miles. It was during this wet period that the first stages of the food economy that led to agriculture began. Dances that were performed to appease the heavens in an effort to facilitate food abundance are witnessed on millennia-old rock paintings and engravings produced during the era.

Africa's Climates Today

It is important to note, there is no such thing as an "African environment." Every climatic condition possible on earth, can be witnessed in Africa. Mediterranean climates are mild with predictable rainfall during the winter months, and a dry climate in the summer. Africa has two such regions, one in the northern tip and one in the southeast area of the continent. The Sahara Desert in the north is the largest in the world and encompasses almost the entire top half of the continent. The Kalahari Desert is located in the southern portion of the continent and convers much of Botswana, parts of Namibia, and areas of South Africa.

The Nile on the eastern region of the continent is the longest river in the world. Mountains in Africa include Mt. Kilimanjaro,

Mt. Kenya, and the Atlas Mountains in Morocco. These mountaintop regions contain ski areas, ice climbing, and glaciers. The southern tip of Africa supports a population of penguins.

The closer one travels to the equator, wetter and more forested terrains are witnessed. Alternatively, as one travels further from the equator the environment becomes drier and grassier – except for the desert which contains little grass in some areas and no grass at all in others. Despite popular notions, few jungles exist in Africa. Rather, the continent is replete with rainforests. Over the past ten thousand years the rainforests in West Africa have undergone several cycles of contraction and expansion.

The continent of Africa straddles the equator. Subsequently, patterns in Africa's terrain due to climatic change are witnessed on a north-south orientation.

- Mediterranean
- Desert
- Savannah
- Rainforest
- Rainforest
- Savannah
- Desert
- Mediterranean

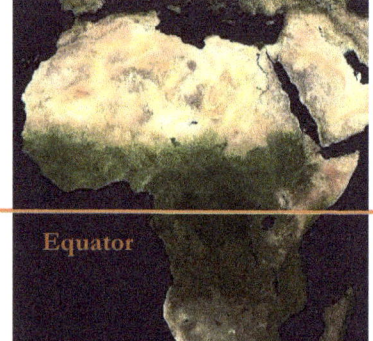

Map 2.2 Africa's Terrain

Map 2.2 displays the effect of the position of the equator and of climate on Africa's landmass. The rainfall, or lack thereof, and specific characteristics of the area such as desert, or rainforest, created a north-south mirror effect with regard to Africa's terrain. Map 2.2 is not drawn to scale.

Africa's Soils

Africa's soils are as diverse as its climates. Due to the heat in areas where the continent has year-round hot weather, the organic materials that nourish the soil decompose all year. Ultimately, those soils are not as rich as farmers would like. Alternatively, volcanic highlands (regions with mountains) are cooler, and thus contain richer soils. Regions with volcanic highlands include Ethiopia, Kenya, Tanzania, Rwanda, Burundi, Uganda, Democratic Republic of the Congo and Cameroon.

The amount of rain a territory receives in Africa is affected by the Intertropical Convergence Zone (ITCZ). The ITCZ is also referred to as the rain belt, a boundary where the dry continental air over the desert converges with the wet air over the ocean. As the rain belt moves from north to south, the area it passes over receives rain. The rain belt moves from north to south yearly as wind patterns change. Its timing is variable therefore rainfall is irregular. When the rain belt retreats early, the most northern regions fail to receive rain.

The climate in Africa dictates the migrations of people and the types of culture and dances they produce. It determines the political and social institutions developed, and the types of diets and lifestyles adopted by the diverse ethnicities and nations of people on the continent. Accordingly, systems and techniques for food acquisition were historically and are presently based on the climatic situations of particular terrains. Thus, dances were developed to ensure food security among other things, in specific environments.

The Map of Africa

Currently, Africa is comprised of over fifty-four countries and territories including its surrounding islands. The newest country is South Sudan, which became an independent nation on July 9, 2011 when it split from Northern Sudan (also referred to as the Republic of Sudan). The country borders on the continent of Africa were artificially created via the colonial conquest. Consequently, African countries currently witnessed were created in the late nineteenth century. The key to identifying the locations of ancient cultural systems, empires, states, and polities, is to study Africa's rivers and bodies of water, and obtaining a keen knowledge of geographical changes that occurred through the ages.

The lands are distributed around and divided by bodies of water. Additionally, the rivers and bodies of land during specific eras differed from their current appearance. As discussed earlier, fifteen thousand years ago, the Sahara desert was lush wetland that supported abundant plant life and animals. Accordingly, the bodies of water that existed during the periods under study should be examined, but the current bodies of water are a good starting point. For example, twenty thousand years ago Lake Chad was a Mega-lake. For a notion of where it was located in Africa at that time, one would need knowledge of where the small Lake Chad is located currently on the continent and estimate its growth in size from that point.

For the purposes of this study, it would be advantageous to be familiar with specific major rivers and bodies of water that currently exist in Africa (see Table 2.1).

Table 2.1 Rivers and Bodies of Water in Africa

The Senegal River	The Niger River	Lake Victoria
The Nile River	The Volta River	Lake Chad
The Congo River	The Orange River	Kasai River
The Zambezi River	The Limpopo River	Lake Kivu

Table 2.1 lists Rivers and Bodies of Water in Africa that are significant to this study.

Although Africa contains many more bodies of water than what is depicted in Table 2.1, the locations of these particular bodies of water and the lands that surround them will facilitate understanding of the placement of historic accounts in specific areas on the continent of Africa discussed in this work. Thus, the rivers and lakes can be used as landmarks to identify cultural phenomena that occurred prior to the nineteenth century. One should also familiarize oneself with specific "landmark" territories such as: the Sahara Desert, the Kalahari Desert, and the Sahel.

Southern Africa

3 Southern Africa

The effects of climate on the diverse terrains in Africa were discussed in chapter 2. However, it must not be misconstrued that developments in Africa over time are limited to land and climate. Large and small migrations of people through the ages have equally impacted the cultures and societies found on the continent. Research on the types of dances produced before, during, and after these migratory periods would provide rich insights on ancient and contemporary cultures and the peoples that created them. Our discussion on African dance history will therefore begin with one of the most ancient cultures in Africa, the San.

The San

Southern Africa was first inhabited by the San. Historically, they resided in an area that spanned seven countries in Southern Africa. In the early part of the first century CE, the Khoikhoi began to migrate into the Southern African region. Over time, cultural anthropologists and historians began to refer to the two groups of people collectively as Khoisan. It is important to note, the Khoikhoi are traditionally pastoralists, the San are traditionally foragers (also referred to as hunters and gathers). Although the Khoikhoi refers to a specific ethnicity, the appellation 'San' describes a group of nations with distinct ethnicities that share historic and linguistic tenets and have

22 *Southern Africa*

Map 3.1 Southern Africa

Within the black circle, Map 3.1 displays the area that will be considered Southern Africa in this study. Although other neighboring countries such as Angola have been considered to be part of Southern African in other studies, for our purposes, we will restrict ourselves to the area indicated. [6]

---

[6] For a different designation for the Southern Africa region see, *Compact Atlas of the World: Digital Mapping for the 21st Century* (London: Jonathan Metcalf, 2009), 56-7.

adopted a specific lifestyle and food economy. Accordingly, although the two groups are often discussed as one, our historical study of dance in Africa will begin with an ethnic group belonging to the San, but not the Khoikhoi. It is important to note that the San groups, the Khoikhoi, and the BaNtu are African peoples engaged in cultural practices indicative of their African origin. Historically – and lingering to present day – European scholars have separated the San and Khoikhoi from Africans of the BaNtu language group. The rationale – if one can call the explanation rational – was the skin color of the San and the Khoikhoi was of a lighter hue. Such scholarship has been dispensed with for the most part in academia, but it still lingers in a few areas of research and scholarship.[7] The diversity on the continent of Africa includes its peoples and precludes the notion of a 'typical' African appearance. From the nearly eight-foot Watutsi to the less than five-foot-tall Twa, and from the light complexioned Berber to the darker skinned Southern Sudanese, diversity abounds in Africa. One clear indication of such diversity is the range of complexions.

The San include such nations as Tsoa, Jul'hoan, !Kung and many others totaling some thirty-five linguistic groups. Traditionally they primarily resided in southern Africa in Botswana, Namibia, Zambia, South Africa, Lesotho, and Zimbabwe, but San nations may also be found in Angola, Mozambique and other parts of Africa currently. They employ a click sound in the numerous dialects they speak.[8] According to geneticists, the San's gene pattern is ancient, and they are direct

---

[7] For a recent example of European scholars differentiating between San and BaNtu based on skin color see David Lewis-Williams and Sam Callis, *Deciphering Ancient Minds: The Mystery of San Bushman Rock Art* (London: Thames & Hudson, 2011), 35.
[8] When the BaNtu migrated to the Southern African region San nations preceded them. Although the BaNtu presently outnumber the San, there is evidence of cultural borrowing via the number of clicking sounds identified within the BaNtu language.

descendants of the world's oldest humans.⁹ The San provided subsistence for themselves via the collection of vegetation, nuts, and roots, and they hunted small animals. Due to the nature of their food economy system, they constantly traveled to different locales to gather vegetables, roots, and so on, wherever vegetation may be found during the year. Consequently, the San did not construct permanent residencies and they only retained the tools and necessary items they needed for survival.¹⁰ They did not accumulate private property and regarded sharing as not only noble but the duty of all in the group. Their societies were without stratification and were based on egalitarian principles.¹¹ Thus, there was no office of the chief, only lineage or clan elders. Decisions were arrived at through majority consent. Disagreements were resolved through lengthy group discussion. The San traveled in small groups of twenty-five to fifty people.

Enter the BaNtu

The BaNtu is a large subcategory of the Niger-Congo language group in Africa.¹² Thus, it is not a single ethnic group or lineage

---

⁹ For an extensive discussion on the genetic African origins of humans see, Spencer Wells, *The Journey of Man: A Genetic Odyssey* (Princeton: Princeton University Press, 2017).

¹⁰ The San constructed temporary shelters in the summer and shelters around waterholes in the winter during their travels. The winter shelters were utilized for longer periods of time than the summer shelters.

¹¹ Societies exhibit stratification when they are structured on a hierarchical foundation with the centralized governing authority at the top and several layers of authority beneath it in a descending order of power.

¹² There are four language classifications in Africa: Afro-Asiatic; Khoisan; Niger-Congo; and Nilo-Saharan. Languages were grouped according to similar root traits among other things. See Bernard Heine and Derek Nurse, eds., *African Languages: An Introduction* (Cambridge: Cambridge University Press, 2000).

of people. Linguists have noticed that the languages – with the exception of Khoisan – spoken by the countless ethnicities and lineages from Cameroon to the East coast of Africa and from Central African Republic to the tip of South Africa, are closely related. Thus, the Wolof language spoken in Senegal in the Western most portion of Africa is related to Zulu spoken at the furthest point south on the continent. As a result of this commonality, linguists employed the word common to most of the languages in the group, *ntu*, which means "person," and connected *ba*, the common plural form for words in this colossal language grouping. Subsequently, they formed the word BaNtu.[13] It comprises the largest grouping in the Niger-Congo language group. The BaNtu language group matured in West Africa before it expanded to other areas in the African continent.

Three major periods of BaNtu expansion are witnessed. The southward migrations of the BaNtu occurred from roughly 3500-2000 BCE.[14] Between 2500-2000 BCE, the BaNtu's expansion exponentially increased for reasons presently unknown to historians. The BaNtu expansion brought agriculture, fishing, tool technology and living in settlements to areas that were previously dominated by nomadic foragers.

As the BaNtu spread through Southern Africa, they either absorbed, drove out, or lived beside the indigenous San. More important, cultural traits were borrowed by each group. This is significant since dance is part and parcel of culture.

---

[13] It is also spelled with lower case letters and only the first letter capitalized, "Bantu." However, this study will capitalize the first letter in each of the words that comprise the resulting compound.

[14] The BaNtu's migrations South and East from their original West African homelands were gradually executed in three waves that are recognized as major periods by historians. First major period – 3000s BCE; second major period – 2000s BCE; third major period – 1000s BCE. The BaNtu migration to the Southern African region occurred between the first and second major period. See Christopher Ehret, *The Civilizations of Africa: A History to 1800* (Charlottesville: University of Virginia Press, 2016), 106-16.

The !Kung Healing Dance

The !Kung healing dance commences in the evening. It begins with women singing "medicine" songs.[15] Such songs contain *n/um*, a spiritual potency that exists in the cosmos, the shamans, and in large animals, thus, forming a connective thread that resonates through the shamans, the spirit world and the earth.[16] Men and women are shamans in !Kung culture, however, medicine songs are often sung by the women. While singing the medicine songs, women form a dance circle and they light a fire in the center.[17] The dance circle is comprised of the women's bodies. Once the women's singing begins to build momentum, the men retrieve their dancing rattles, tie them to their legs and dance around the women creating a protective circle. The rhythmic movements of the dance, the repetitive vibrations of the songs, and the percussive sounds of the clapping alter the dancer's state of mind and ushers it into what's referred to as half-death. While in the half-death mind state, the dancers dance toward individuals with aliments, lay hands on them and draws the illness out of them.

The healing dance employs copious foot percussive movements (see Figure 3.2). The rhythmic patterns made with

---

[15] Medicine songs are sung to initiate physical, spiritual, emotional, or mental healing.

[16] Spiritual potency or power is known as n/um. The existence of n/um in medicine songs differentiate them from recreational and other social songs. Shamans are people who have access to the spirit world and serve as intermediaries for laymen to engage the cosmos. See Ester A. Dagan, ed., *The Spirit's Dance in Africa: Evolution, Transformation, and Continuity in Sub-Sahara* (Quebec: Galerie Amrad African Arts Publications, 1997), 36.

[17] Dance circles are witnessed throughout Africa and in the African diaspora via the transatlantic slave trade when enslaved Africans brought their culture to the Americas. For a discussion on dance circles in Africa see, Ofosuwa M. Abiola, *History Dances: Chronicling the History of Traditional Mandinka Dance* (London: Routledge, 2019), 75-6.

Southern Africa 27

Figure 3.1 !Kung Healing Dance
Photograph: Aga Szydlick

Figure 3.2 !Kung Healer
Photograph: Khwe

the feet and the sounds of the dancing rattles tied to the dancer's legs facilitate the half-death trance state and the relief felt by those seeking healing. Currently, in addition to experiencing the !Kung healing dance live, this dance and other San dances live on through their depiction on rock art millennia old in Southern Africa.

Rock Art: The Oldest Documentation of Dance

Rock art is the collective name for ancient paintings and engravings found on rocks, in caves, on mountain cliffs, and hillsides. Rock art has been found in every region on the continent of Africa. The oldest specimen of deliberate etching or drawing on rock in the world was discovered in South Africa in Blombos Cave and is dated seventy-three thousand years old.[18] Rock art has been used to document dance for millennia by ancient people in Africa.

San rock art reveals much about their traditional dances and way of life. Presently, there are fourteen thousand documented San rock art sites in southern Africa and archeologists expect to discover countless more. In addition to hunting and other scenes in everyday life, San dance rituals were copiously recorded on rock art. For example, there are many instances of the !Kung healing dance portrayed on San rock art. Illustrations depict the dance circle comprised of healers singing and clapping while dancing. Those forming the dance circle are also holding spears and some are sometimes wearing white face paint. Despite the age of the rock art, the dancers' rituals, attire, face paint, and significant objects are vividly depicted and finely detailed. In addition to rock art, other types of evidence can also

---

[18] See Christopher S. Henshilwood et al., "An abstract drawing from the 73,000-year-old levels at Blombos Cave, South Africa" *Nature* (2018): 115-18.

Figure 3.3 San Dance Ritual
Drakensberg Mountains, South Africa

Figure 3.3 depicts a San dance ceremony where women are standing on the left and the right clapping and probably chanting. Men are positioned in the middle leaning on sticks while performing the stick dance.

Figure 3.4 San Healing Dance
Drakensberg Mountains, South Africa

Figure 3.4 illustrates a version of the Healing dance. The sick person is positioned in the middle along with the healer. Participants in the healing process are positioned outside of the circle clapping, chanting, and raising spears to aid the healing ceremony.

provide a lens through which ancient cultural practices can be understood today.

The Nyungwe of Mozambique

In a limestone cave near Lake Niassa in Mozambique, the earliest direct evidence in the world, of human beings utilizing pre-domesticated cereals was found. In 2007, dozens of one hundred thousand-year-old stone tools were recovered.[19] The historic find confirmed that humans in what is now modern-day Mozambique consumed wild sorghum. Currently, sorghum is widely used in Africa for porridges, breads, flours and alcoholic beverages. This historic recovery also revealed that ancient humans in Mozambique also consumed the false banana, wild oranges, palm wine, and the African "potato."[20] The types of food economy employed by peoples in the past informs us about the nature of the dances fashioned, the type of materials available for dance attire and for body paint, and the kinds of materials available for props and textiles. For example, agricultural dances tend to include movement vocabulary with low torsos and bent knees – movements naturally performed when planting and harvesting seeds. Areas where grasses are available for food (all grains are from the agricultural family of grasses) dance attire often includes grass skirts and ankle or calf ornaments, and grass or a raffia type material on the masks.

In Mozambique, San foragers were the first to inhabit the country but by 500 CE, the BaNtu had migrated into the area. It is assumed that the ancient San were the peoples that consumed

---

[19] Julio Mercader, "Mozambican Grass Seed Consumption During the Middle Stone Age," *Science* 326, no. 5960 (December 18, 2009): 1680-1683, accessed June 21, 2019, www.sciencedaily.com/releases/2009/12/091217141312.htm.

[20] Enset is a plant that resembles the banana plant, hence the name "false banana."

Southern Africa 31

Map 3.2 Mozambique

Mozambique's border length is substantial extending the country from lower central to southern Africa. As a consequence, it is often considered in discussions on East Africa. For our purposes, Mozambique will be discussed in a Southern Africa context.

the wild sorghum discussed earlier. However, the practice of wild sorghum consumption was obviously borrowed by more recent migrants into the area, hence its widespread use in Southern Africa and the rest of the continent.

The Nyungwe are a BaNtu people presently located in Mozambique generally, and in high concentrations in the Tete Province along the Zambezi River. The Nyungwe also reside in Zimbabwe and other areas in Southern Africa, but it is the Nyungwe of the Tete Providence that have become famous for their traditional Nyanga flute dances.

Nyanga Flute Dance

The nyanga flute dance is a complex foot percussive dance performed simultaneously while playing flutes, or nyanga, and singing. Men and women perform it in a circle.[21] Nyanga flutes are constructed from bamboo or sometimes from reeds. Round bamboo stalks of different circumferences and distinct lengths are tied together and played as one instrument. Each stalk produces a different sound than the stalks tied on either side of it. Nyanga musicians play the flutes by blowing into different bamboo stalks in a pattern that produces a melody. The voice is also used intermittently between blows to enhance and contribute to the sound. In addition to the flute players, other participants shake handheld rattles while they also use their voices in chants and harmony to enhance the sound. The handheld rattles are long in the middle and round at the top and

---

[21] Many scholars refer to flutes constructed from bamboo or reeds as panpipes. Pan is a Greek god known in mythology for playing reed flutes. Hence, nyanga flutes are also known as "Nyanga Panpipes." For an extensive discussion on the nyanga flute dance see, Andrew Tracey, "The Nyanga Panpipe Dance," in *African Music: Journal of the International Library of African Music* Vol. 5, no. 1 (July 1971). Accessed April 20, 2019. http://journal.ru.ac.za/index.php/africanmusic/article/view/1152.

Figure 3.5 Ritual Nyanga Dance, Nyengwe Community, Zambezi Valley, Mozambique.

Image: City of Music Project, Minister of Culture, Mozambique, 2011.

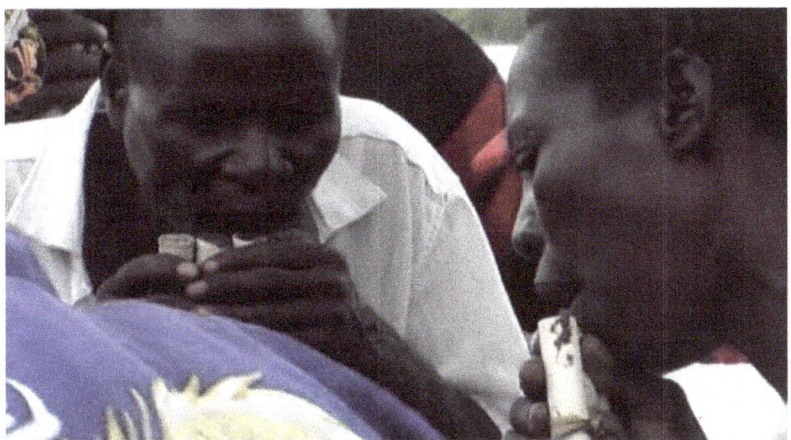

Figure 3.6 Playing Nyanga, Nyengwe Community, Zambezi Valley, Mozambique.

Image: City of Music Project, Minister of Culture, Mozambique, 2011.

Figures 3.5 and 3.6 display the performance of a nyanga flute dance. Notice that when dancing, the practitioners hold their torsos in acute angles at the high to medium positions.

the bottom. A handle protrudes from the bottom to enable the player to grip and manipulate it while playing.

Complex percussive dance steps are performed during the singing and chanting and while the Nyanga flutes and handheld rattles are played. Three long metal rattles are tied together and tied onto the bottom of the right leg in the area of the calves of the dancers. The dance steps are highly percussive, and employs syncopated steps along with hops, shuffles, marches, turns into and out of the circle, swinging the stomping leg back and forth, and glides, among other steps. The dancers execute dance phrases in unison and each phrase performed has a distinct name. The dance is performed via an interval of dancing, singing, and playing the flutes and rattles, followed by an interval of chanting, singing or calling without the flute playing. The non-playing nyanga flute interval lasts for six counts and the flute-playing interval continues for twelve counts. A different dance phrase is performed during each flute-playing interval. During the non-flute playing interval, dancers move in a counterclockwise direction performing a march step emphasizing the leg with the rattles (the right leg). The lead singer chants, sings, or sometimes calls the next dance phrase. He or she has six counts to do such. Afterwards the nyanga flute-playing, singing, and dance begins once again for twelve counts. There are nyanga flute dances for myriad occasions. For example, there is a nyanga flute dance performed to make rain during droughts.

Northern Africa

4   Northern Africa

Perhaps more than any other territory on the African continent, northern Africa has undergone significant climatic and geologic change. The Sahara Desert, the largest in the world, was once a lush vegetated region teeming with animals and bodies of water. The resulting changes in population density in the region also serve as a testament to the immense changes witnessed in north Africa. Populations of people as far away as West Africa testify to their origins in Northeast Africa.[22] North Africa is also one of the first regions on the continent to be invaded my Arabs from the Middle East. As a consequence, Islam became the state religions of all polities in the Northern portion of Africa.

Egyptian Dance from Nubian Culture

Archeological evidence reveals that Egyptian culture, political systems, ideology, religions, and so on, originated in Nubia which was located in Sub-Saharan Africa. From there, it spread to Southern Egypt, and then to Northern Egypt. Nubian culture spread north to Southern Egypt in circa 3300 BCE. The original diverse polities of proto-Egypt were unified in 3100 BCE by king (or Pharaoh) Menes (also known as Namer). The unification had significant effects on the culture overall. However, the most

---

[22] While interviewing a Fulani dancer in The Gambia, he disclosed to me that his family line originated in Egypt. Generations of migrations resulted in their present residence in The Gambia.

Map 4.1 Northern Africa

Northern Africa spans from Morocco to Egypt. Although Morocco is located to the far West, notice that it is positioned in the North of the continent. The Arabic name, Maghreb, or "place where the sun sets" in English (i.e. the West), was given to the country by early Arab explorers.

obvious changes were witnessed in the religious systems of the new state. Nubian religions were originally monotheistic.[23] As a result of the unification, and in an effort to promote amicability among the diverse kingdoms brought together, Egyptian religion became polytheistic. The smaller kingdom's gods were given a voice, and subsequently, an ideological and cultural stake in the new state. However, after Egypt's unification, the Nubian religions that were adopted by the new state became polytheistic. Kings began to be deified. That is, they became divine kings that, after death would take their place with the gods. The first dance systems in Egypt were performed as an expression of religious devotion. Thus, early Egyptian rituals and ceremonies virtually always included dance and the essential core of those dances were Nubian in nature. Over time, the dance styles were adopted to the circumstances in the newly unified Egypt. To fully appreciate the changes the dances underwent, fundamental knowledge of Egypt's history is needed.

Egyptian History: A Brief Overview

Egypt experienced several significant periods. Egyptologists have categorized historic eras in Egypt into three branches, the Old Kingdom, the Middle Kingdom, and the New Kingdom.

---

[23] It is not known what people in remote eras of history referred to themselves as. To piece together the cultural practices of specific peoples, historians, linguists, and archaeologists utilize language groups or sometimes a distinctive pervasive tenet in the culture of the people studied. In the millennia prior the unification of Egypt, one of the names scholars applied to the people of the Nile region was "Sudanic." For early pre-Egypt unification religious practices of Sudanic people, see Christopher Ehret, *The Civilizations of Africa: A History to 1800* (Charlottesville: University of Virginia Press, 2016), 14.

Each of these periods were characterized by specific dynasties.[24] The era before the unification of Egypt is the predynastic period.

The Old Kingdom spanned from 3100 to 2300 BCE. During this era, it was believed that pyramids were the only tombs appropriate for a king. Step pyramids were initially invented, but later, the steps were disposed of and pyramids with smooth sloping sides became the standard. During the Old Kingdom, the three largest pyramids ever built were constructed. They were built for Khufu, his son, and grandson at Giza. The Old Kingdom ended with Pharaoh Pepi II's death.

At the decline of ruling dynasties, and before the commencement of new ones, a period of chaos and disorganization occurred. Egypt experienced two such periods, historically referred to as the first and second intermediate periods respectively. The first intermediate period began shortly after Pharaoh Pepi's death, from 2280 to 2050 BCE. Thus, the Middle Kingdom began in roughly 2050 BCE.

The Middle Kingdom ended in the 1780s BCE. Due to internal conflict and lack of strong leadership, by the 1790s the second intermediate period had begun. During this time of turmoil, the Hyksos, a people from Western Asia, invaded the northern half of Egypt. The Intermediate Period ended in the 1590s BCE, when Ahmose I defeated and drove out the Hyksos. Ahmose I restored Egypt's sovereignty, founded a new dynasty, and became the first pharaoh of the eighteenth dynasty and the New Kingdom.

The Particulars of Egyptian Dance

Dance was a significant profession in ancient Egypt. It was the dominant element in cultural events throughout all dynasties.

---

[24] A dynasty is a family of or line of hereditary rulers of a country.

The movement vocabulary of the dancers was substantial. In addition to running movements, leaps, acrobatic movements, knee bends, leg extensions, among other things, ancient Egyptian dancers are depicted on pyramid walls and papyrus executing pirouettes or turns.[25] Professional dancers were either freelance or they were affiliated with a temple, estate, or a royal lineage. Gradually, many cultural elements that began as solely a priest and aristocrat class privilege, eventually made their way down to the laymen class. As a result, dancemaking occurred in diverse social groups and classes in ancient Egypt. The purpose for dance also expanded. Thus, there were religious dances, dances performed for entertainment, dances performed during times of war, theatrical, ceremonial and festive dances, agricultural and metalsmith dances, and so on.

The standard form of entertainment after dinner for the aristocrats was the all-female dance ensemble. On papyrus and tomb drawings, the after-dinner dance is depicted as a court dance performed in the palace. However, no evidence has been unearthed thus far that precludes the possibility of such events also occurring in the homes of the laymen. Additionally, dance was not reserved solely for women. Occasions arose where it was necessary for groups of male and female dancers to perform. Alternatively, the pyramid walls and substantial specimens of papyrus display all male dance ensembles or solos as well.

Religious dance was a part of life before dance moved to its esteemed place in secular circles. For example, there were all male funeral dance troupes known as Muu. The Muu represents the earthly water and the earthly reflection of the heavenly waters. Muu dancers often wore tall reed head pieces to

---

[25] Lesley Kinney provides a comprehensive study on ancient Egyptian dance in *Dance, Dancers and the Performance Cohort in the Old Kingdom* (Oxford: BAR Publishing, 2016). Kinney provides a detailed examination of Egyptian dance and sheds light on much of ancient Egypt's movement vocabulary.

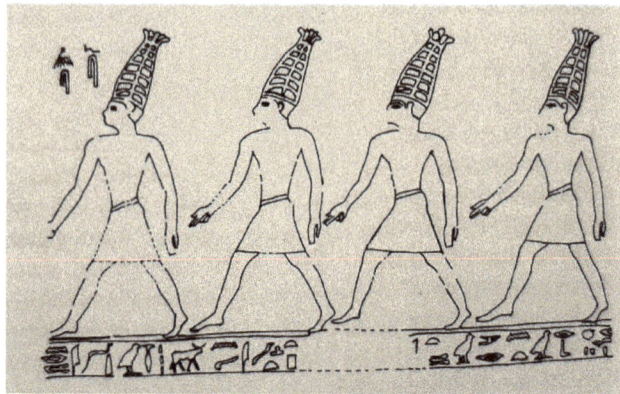

Figure 4.1 Two pairs of Muu Dancers

Figure 4.2 A Pair of Muu Dancers

Figures 4.1 and 4.2 depict Muu dancers. Notice that Muu dancers perform in even numbered groups of men to facilitate dancing in pairs. Often, the dancers wear long reeds on their heads derived from locations surrounding the bodies of water where the plant grows. The type of reed worn is determined by the region where the dance is performed.

symbolize the relationship with the earthly and celestial water. Muu dance groups were comprised of pairs of male dancers. They moved in unison but performed the dance movements as mirror reflections of each other.[26]

Most if not all ancient dance in Egypt was religious in nature and a combination of dance and theatre. To date, the oldest documented source of dance theatre in Egypt is dated at 2600 BCE. The Ramesseum Dramatic Papyrus denotes the name of the drama and the medium it is written on. It is an account of the coronation of Senusret I. The Ramesseum Drama was written by the master of ceremony, Ikhernofret. The script of the coronation ritual is quite detailed and contains illustrations of dances, scenes, dialog spoken by actors representing various gods, stage directions, and so on.

The temple reliefs at Edfu contain a text of a religious drama that occurred during the New Kingdom. It was performed at the Heru festival while a statute of the goddess Het Heru was carried from her temple at Dendera to the festival at Edfu. In the text, ballet scenes and symbolic dances were described. Stage directions for a large number of dancers, actors, props, statutes, backdrops, and even extras were also mentioned. Women dancers – and other women – in ancient Egypt wore cowrie shells and waist beads. Waist beads were – and still are – a traditional ornament worn by women in Africa under their clothes for various purposes including rite of passage, alluring their mates, healing ceremonies, and so on.

Although dance training is not generally depicted on tombs and papyrus discovered thus far, secular professional training probably occurred via an apprenticeship process. On a secular non-professional level, children probably began dancing very young emulating family members. Religious dance was

---

[26] See Lesley Kinney, *Dance, Dancers and the Performance Cohort in the Old Kingdom* (1809; repr., Oxford: BAR Publishing, 2016), 122-23.

probably taught in their religious schools along with other physical, intellectual, and spiritual skills. Sub-Saharan cultural influences formed the foundation of ancient Egyptian dance systems. Similarly, on the other side of Africa to the far west and in more recent times, Sub-Saharan cultural influences also significantly impacted a society in the North.

The Gnawa: History, Culture and Dance

The Gnawa (also spelled Gnaoua), an ethnic group in Morocco (and other parts of North Africa), are originally from the Western Sahel region and localities south of it, in West Africa.[27] They primarily hail from territories that existed where Mali, Senegal, The Gambia, Burkina Faso, and Niger are currently located. However, oral tradition testifies to the fact that Gnawa were also transported from as far away as northern Nigeria, among other places. To comprehend Gnawa dance and culture, their foundational history must be engaged, a history that begins with the expansion of Islam into Northwest Africa.

After Islam emerged in the Middle East in the seventh century, Muslims invaded North Africa and spread to the far west to Morocco. They imposed Islam as the state religions of all the lands they conquered in north Africa – Algeria, Morocco, Libya, Egypt, and Tunisia. The western branch of the Muslim invasion in North Africa is referred to as the Maghreb.

The Arab Muslims attempted to spread south to the Senegambia region to gain control of the large deposits of gold there. However, the empires and kingdoms in the Senegambia

---

[27] The Sahel is the region of Africa located directly beneath the arid Sahara Desert and spans to just above the humid savannas. It forms a transitional zone between the desert and the savanna and rainforests. The Sahel stretches across the entire continent of Africa from Senegal in the west to the Sudan in the east. Gnawa also reside in Algeria, Libya, and Tunisia.

Northern Africa 45

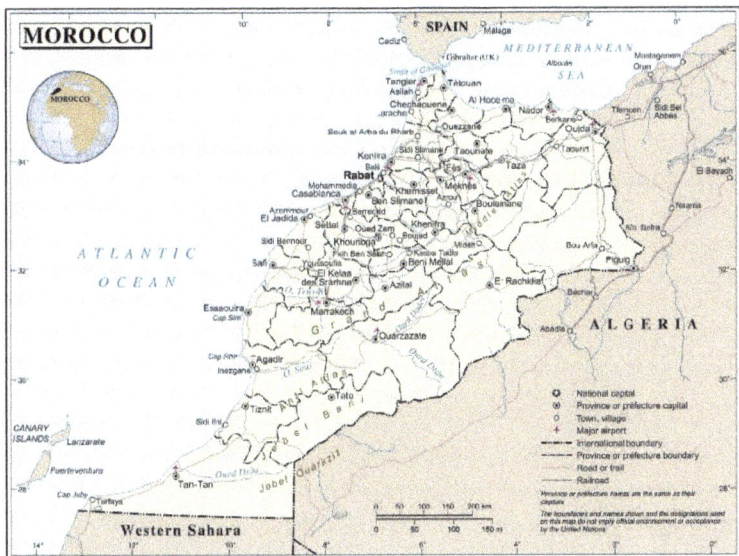

Map 4.2 Political Map of Morocco

Map 4.2 depicts the current borders of the Kingdom of Morocco (oval circle). Map 4.3 portrays the Western Sahel or Senegambia (black square), and its distance from Morocco. Thus, the Gnawa are comprised of diverse ethnicities emanating from localities across the Sahara Desert.

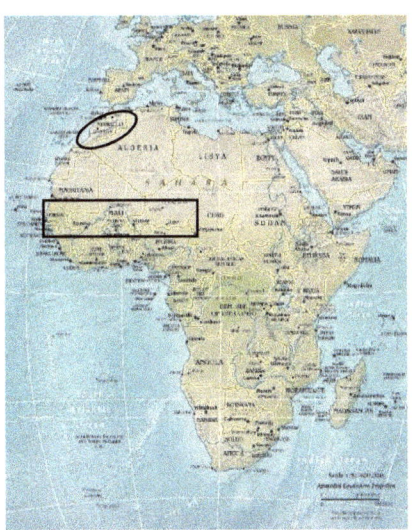

Map 4.3 Morocco and Western Sudan

region during the initial conquests of north Africa were too formidable for the Muslims to overpower.[28] Over time, due to a variety of internal and external factors, by the sixteenth century, these Senegambian empires and kingdoms had begun to weaken.

Songhai emerged in the Western Sahel in the 1400s after the decline of the Mali Empire. It became the largest and most powerful of the Sub-Saharan empires of the era, yet in 1590, civil strife began to manifest. The Moroccan sultan, Amhad al-Mansur, in 1591, took advantage of Songhai's unfortunate civil circumstances. He invaded Songhai, was victorious, but was only able to hold on to control of it for a few decades.

The Moroccan-Songhai war resulted in numerous Senegambian prisoners of war transported to Morocco as slaves. Although slaves were utilized in many aspects of Moroccan society – assistants, cooks, husbandry, and so on – many of the enslaved Africans from Senegambia during al-Mansur's reign were placed in the military and became one of al-Mansur's personal royal guards. Later, these personal guards became the official Moroccan military and were referred to as the Black Guard. This cycle continued with subsequent Moroccan and North African leaders.[29] The practice became standardized and

---

[28] Senegambia in this sense refers to the common culture of the people that resided in territories between and outside of the Senegal, the Gambia and the Niger Rivers. The borders that delimit the modern countries of Senegal and The Gambia were created in the nineteenth century via the imposition of colonialism. Empires in the Senegambia region at the time of the Arab invasion in the north were Ancient Ghana, Tekrur, Mali, Songhai, and Gao among others. These empires were ruled by formidable kings with powerful armies.

[29] Enslaved Senegambian women were transported to Morocco to marry the soldiers in the Black Guard. Their male children were trained for service in the military and female children were taught domestic chores. Colonies or territories were set aside for these Senegambian families. Although this study focuses on Morocco, after the Arab conquest of North Africa, Morocco was only one of many Islamized North and East African and Middle Eastern

by the nineteenth century, the sultan Moulay Ismail is reputed to have obtained one hundred fifty thousand enslaved Senegambian men to staff his military, and one hundred fifty thousand Senegambian women to serve as wives for his Black soldiers.

As mentioned earlier, the military was not the only area of Moroccan society where Sub-Saharan enslaved Africans were stationed. As a result of the large numbers of Senegambians present in Morocco over time, a subculture gradually emerged with memories and traditions of the homelands they were forced to abandon. The progenitors of this subculture are the Gnawa. The Gnawa is primarily comprised of people from the Fulani, Mandinka, Bambara, Soninke nations, but oral tradition attests to the inclusion of Hausas and other groups in smaller numbers.

Songs of History

Gnawa culture contains sacred and secular dances and their songs are the driving force for both types of dances. The journey across the Sahara Desert was just as horrific and often as fatal as crossing the Atlantic Ocean during the transatlantic slave trade centuries later. Thus, a prolific amount of Gnawa songs speak of the injustices their ancestors endured throughout the trans-Saharan slave trade era. Other types of songs that are abundantly sung are religious in nature.

Not unlike people of African descent in America, the Caribbean, and other parts of the world, the Gnawa refer to themselves as part of the African Diaspora. Although they

---

states that practiced this form of slavery. For an extensive discussion on Morocco's enslaved Senegambians see, Chouki *El Hamel, Black Morocco: A History of Slavery, Race, and Islam* (Cambridge: Cambridge University Press, 2013).

Figure 4.3 Gnawa at Marrakesh Market, Morocco, 2010

Photograph: Kevin Ealey

Figure 4.3 depicts the author making a purchase from a Gnawa dancer-musician at Marrakesh Market, Morocco. Notice the distinctive cowrie shell studded sash and fez with the tassel hanging in the back. The dancer is holding krakebs, a traditional Gnawa instrument played similar to castanets.

originate on the same continent they were enslaved on, the Gnawa assert that they were involuntarily transported via the trans-Saharan slave trade, and were dispersed to other areas of Africa, Europe, and the Middle East. Thus, they are part of the African Diaspora.

Music, Dress, and Africanized Islam

Islam was imposed on the Gnawa simultaneously with their enslavement. Yet, they practice a form of Islam that allows for indigenous African rituals or what scholars refer to as Africanized Islam.[30] The sect of Islam that is most receptive to African indigenous tenets is the Sufi branch of Islam. Sufism has long been recognized as the form of Islam that embraces and practices mysticism as part of its normal customs.

Since Gnawa traditional dance and music are part and parcel of their culture, it was brought into their practice of Sufism. However, the same movement vocabulary and dance phrases are witnessed in Gnawa secular dance as well. Although the rhythms, tempos, and tunes may change in traditional Gnawa music, the use of traditional instruments and attire are constant in sacred and secular ceremonies and events.

Specific instruments are used in Gnawa music. Krakebs are iron castanets that are round at each end but narrow in the middle. They are handheld and include a strap that facilitates maneuvering with the hands. The distinctive sound made by the krakebs symbolize the hooves of horses striking the ground as their ancestors were carried away to be enslaved, and the eerie sound of the shackles used to restrain their people. They are also

---

[30] Africanized Islam is a term Africanist scholars use to describe the incorporation of traditional African religious tenets in the practice of Islam.

used to enlist help from the world of the unseen.[31] The three-string guitar-like instrument associated with the Gnawa is the guembri. Many of the musical phrases played by the guembri in Gnawa music are similar to those in African American jazz. Tbels are large round drums also used in Gnawa music. They provide the bass rhythm for the dances, are played with a stick-and-hand technique and are worn via a strap across the shoulder. Often the straps are generously decorated with cowrie shells.[32]

Gnawa traditional dress can be identified by the long sashes with abundant cowrie shells sewn on which they place over their garments. Cowrie shells are also sewn around their fezzes.[33] Their tunics are often vibrantly colored, and the fabrics utilized range from cottons to textiles with high shine such as satin and rayon. In addition to fezzes, the Gnawa traditionally wear another distinctive cloth hat. Cowrie shells are also sewn onto the front of the cloth hats. Long braided wool hang from the back of the hats giving the appearance of dreadlocks hanging from underneath. The use of cowrie shells provides a clue for the origin of the Gnawa as they are not indigenous to Morocco. They were brought to the area by the enslaved Senegambians during the trans-Saharan slave trade. Cowrie shells are abundant in West Africa and in diverse locations in Central and East Africa below the Sahara Desert. They serve as a symbol for the land of the Gnawa's ancestors.

---

[31] Chouki el Hamel, *Black Morocco: A History of Slavery, Race, and Islam* (Cambridge: Cambridge University Press, 2013), 278.

[32] Cowrie shells have been utilized in Africa south of the Sahara Desert for millennia. Their meaning in the diverse African cultures they are found in is as diverse. The perhaps more well-known use of cowrie shells in West Africa is as currency. Though, they were also used in spiritual systems, as adornment in hair and on clothes, among other things.

[33] A fez is a round tall hat that certain sects of Muslims wear. Sometimes a tassel hangs from the center on the top.

The Spiritual Dances of the Gnawa

Dance is an integral part of religious worship among the Gnawa. A Gnawa dancer is known as *kuyu*. Gnawa dance is characterized by distinctive movement vocabulary including sudden squats with both knees bent and recovery just as quick. The dancer often holds and plays krakebs while he is dancing. The torso or ribcage is not as active as the lower part of the body. However, the head is sometimes moved in circular motions activating a fan spinning effect of the tassel attached to the top of the cowrie shell studded hat or fez. In addition to squats, rhythmic shuffles, and glides, percussive foot taps are performed with the feet. Full body turns are employed and are not restricted to those not drumming. Thus, drummers, singers or chanters, and krakeb players alike, may dance and communicate with each other through movement.

Women and Gnawa Dance

To date, public displays of Gnawa dance are predominated by men. Yet, women also perform Gnawa dance. The *lila* is a religious ceremony that includes dance, music, song, spiritual poetry, chanting, and trance. Traditionally, Gnawa dance was witnessed solely at *lilas* and only those invited to the *lila* were allowed to attend. Women were customarily the *muqadma*, or emcee at the *lila*. Thus, she possessed a keen knowledge of all the dances, songs, and chants of the spiritual system practiced at the *lila*. The *muqadma* must also know everyone in the room. Those who invoked a trance state at the *lila* were usually women, and the trance state was obtained through sacred Gnawa dance.

Figure 4.4 Gnawa Dancer Leaping

Source: "Gnawa Music A Personal Journey" in *The Score*, February 24, 2017, by Tom Pryer

Figure 4.4 showcases Gnawa dance, regalia, and culture. Tbels, krakebs, cowrie shelled sashes and fezzes are featured during a festival in Essaouira, Morocco.

Eastern Africa

5   Eastern Africa

Eastern Africa is comprised of no less geological wonders than earlier discussed areas on the African continent. For example, the East African Rift system is an active continental phenomenon whereby tectonic plates beneath the earth's surface are pulling apart. The Somali plate (comprised of East Africa) is gradually pulling away from main continental African plate. Although the plates are not expected to completely split for millions of years, their movements dictate volcanic activity in the area. The East African Rift system is part of a larger rift system known as the Great Rift Valley and includes parts of the Middle East.

Perhaps Eastern Africa is best known as the location of the discovery of the famous three million-year-old Lucy fossil, and as the birthplace of mankind. Indeed, East Africa has a rich human story to tell as well. For instance, by the eighth century BCE in the city of Yeha, Ethiopia, and the cities of Matara and Sembel, Eritrea, large complex settlements existed in East Africa.[34] The Eritrean cultures, Matara and Sembel, were part of a culture with an even earlier inception than Yeha. The Eritrean cultures were dubbed the Ona Culture and dated to early-to-mid first millennium BCE. Material culture found at both the Ethiopian and the Eritrea sites included sophisticated sculptures, metallurgy and stone masonry. Some items

---

[34] See Graham Connah, *African Civilizations: An Archaeological Perspective* (Cambridge: Cambridge University Press, 2018), 111.

56 Eastern Africa

Map 5.1 Eastern Africa

The countries of Eastern Africa are displayed within the black square border on Map 5.1. It is noteworthy that although Ethiopia is not on the coast currently – it is blocked by Eritrea, Djibouti, Somaliland, and Somalia – historically, it was able to develop strong trade relations with polities across the Red Sea and the Gulf of Aden.

also contained inscriptions and evidence of contact with the Middle East. The culture practiced in Ethiopia today contains apparent elements of the ancient Yeha culture. Our discussion on dance will begin with a culture that directly inherited its tenets from the ancient Ethiopian and Eritrean cultures discussed above.

History, Religion, and Ancient Ethiopia

The Aksumite (also spelled Axum or Aksum) Empire was established in the second century BCE.[35] By 50 CE, the Empire had assumed control of an area represented by modern-day Eritrea and areas of northern Ethiopia, through its high trade activities. By the fourth century, in addition to parts of Eritrea, Aksum grew to include most of contemporary Ethiopia and parts of the Middle East. The rise of Aksum created a new centralized hub for the flow of international trade. As such, the era witnessed Christian merchants and the introduction to Christianity as a religion to the East African polity. Many Christian merchants funneled their goods through Aksum's port city, Adulis. As a result of the immense profits obtained through engaging Christian dominated trade networks, Aksum's ruler, King Ezana, converted to Christianity to gain unimpeded access. This process would be repeated in later years in West Africa when the region is introduced to Islam and its accompanying trade networks. Although an unprecedented bold step – prior Aksumite kings have never converted to a foreign religion in the history of the empire – Aksum remained a powerful centralized state for three hundred years.

---

[35] G. Moktar, ed., *A General History of Africa*, vol. 2. *Ancient Civilizations of Africa* (Berkeley: University of California Press, 1990), 192.

Map 5.2 Map of Ethiopia

Map 5.2 portrays the present borders of Ethiopia. At its height, the Ancient Axumite Empire included Ethiopia and localities in Eritrea, Djibouti, and Sudan.

In the twelfth century, the Zagwe dynasty emerged. It was a Christian polity located in current-day Ethiopia. The emergent kings of the state validated their political positions through conversion to Christianity. Zagwe kings' most well-known accomplishments were building the colossal rock churches of the Lasta region of Ethiopia. King Lalibela was the most famous of the Zagwe kings. The enormity of his rock churches grabbed the attention of the masses (see Figure 5.1). Consequently, a town was named after him to commemorate his architectural accomplishments. In the twelfth century, King Lalibela commissioned the building of eleven monolithic rock churches in an Ethiopian mountainous region approximately four hundred miles (roughly 645 km) from Ethiopia's current capital, Addis Ababa. His goal was to establish a "New Jerusalem" in Aksum after Christian pilgrimages to the Holy Land was obstructed by Muslim conquests of regions in the Middle East. Centuries after the death of King Lalibela and the decline of Aksum, his namesake city remains significant to a vibrant community of Ethiopian Orthodox priests and nuns. Although Christianity was embraced by the ancient Ethiopian polity Aksum, Ethiopian indigenous religious elements were incorporated into the Christian practices. This syncretism was most evident in the dance systems in Ethiopia.

Other foreign religions were introduced to Ethiopia but the Christian church remained powerful and became the primary patron of the arts. By the sixteenth century, the Christian church suppressed any practice of the arts that occurred without its sanction. For example, Bishop Grigentius passed a law prohibiting the public performance of dancers (singers, musicians, and actors as well) that have not received endorsement from the church prior to the performance.[36] The

---

[36] See Jane Plastow, "Ethiopia and Eritrea" in *A History of Theatre in Africa*, edited by Martin Banham (Cambridge: Cambridge University Press, 2004), 193.

Figure 5.1 Rock Church at Lalibela, Ethiopia

penalty for breaking the law was a whipping and one year of harsh labor. To date, other religious influences from antiquity are also still practiced in Ethiopia. Indigenous religions that existed in the region before the introduction of Christianity, Judaism, and Islam, are still practiced.

Ethiopia's National Dance

The national dance of Ethiopia is Eskista. The English translation is "dancing shoulders." Eskista is practiced in northern Ethiopia by the Amhara, Wollo, Gondar, and other ethnic groups. The songs lead the dance and dictates its meaning. For example, there are war songs, work songs, hunting songs, shepherd songs, ritualistic songs, love songs, and so on, that influence the nuances and choice of movement vocabulary in the dance. Eskista is performed for secular and sacred purposes depending on the song. Accordingly, the motives and characteristics of the dance follow the mood and meaning of the song and can therefore be changed during the dance performance.

Despite the fact that the name of the dance is "dancing shoulders," movement vocabulary in Eskista is not restricted to the shoulders. In addition to shoulder movements, the entire torso or ribcage moves forward and backward in vigorous contractions and in time with the accompanying music. The head bobs forward at the discretion of the dancer. Arms are employed in diverse ways or not at all. A dancer may choose to keep the arms positioned with the hands on the hips to emphasize the torso contractions, shoulders, and head bobbing. Eskista is performed by both men and women and the most skilled dancer is appointed the leader of the group.

Although Eskista's roots lie in antiquity, it is performed today to address the innumerable circumstances one may encounter. Though Eskista is performed for sacred ceremonies, since it is the national dance of Ethiopia, it can be witnessed in many social non-sacred events.

Traditionally, four items, the qemis, netela, gabi, and the kuta, are worn throughout Ethiopia and in Eskista performances. The gabi is worn by both men and women. It is a thick large cotton garment used to protect against cold and wind. As such, it is worn during the cold rainy season and at night. During special occasions and when the weather is warmer, men wear a thin shawl, a kuta, and the women wear a white scarf, or netela. Often netelas are elaborately decorated with intermittent gold or silver metallic threads.

Women also traditionally wear qemis – long white cotton robes with gold or silver threads decorating the waistband and the edges. The qemis are made by sewing strips of woven fabric together. Men wear cotton embroidered tunics with loose

Figure 5.2 Eskista Performance, Ethiopia, 2013

Photograph: Ahmed Younis Sif

fitting cotton pants. Both men and women wear sashes which accentuate the Eskista movements confined to the torso and shoulders. Although white is traditionally worn for most ceremonies, the qemis and the tunics and pants can vary in color.

Traditional instruments used in Eskista performances are the krar – a five or six stringed harp-like instrument – lute or mesenko (also spelled masenqo) – a single-stringed violin-like instrument – and keberos or double headed conical drums. The kebero is a traditional drum played in Ethiopia, Eritrea, and Sudan. The drum is constructed from a single hollowed out tree trunk and cow skins attached to both of the open ends. In Ethiopian ceremonies, the kebero's size varies depending on the occasion. Hence, Ethiopian Orthodox Christian liturgical music utilizes large keberos and smaller versions of keberos are used for social celebrations.

Burundi: History and The Arrival of the Tutsi

As discussed earlier, the country borders witnessed in Africa currently were created by European polities during the Berlin conference and its resulting scramble and partitioning of Africa in the late nineteenth century. Existing African nations, ethnicities, and polities were not taken into account often resulting in the split of ethnic groups and historic nations between two or more countries. Burundi, however, is one of the rare cases in Africa where the historic traditional country borders were retained. The ramifications of this phenomenon cannot be overstated.

Burundi's rich history is often buried under copious amounts of publications emphasizing the 1993 and 1994 genocidal activities in Burundi and Rwanda respectively. Instead, our focus will be on one of the many rich cultural tenets of the country. There are two primary ethnic groups that represent the majority in Burundi, the Hutu which holds the ethnic majority, and the Tutsi (also referred to as the Batutsi). Minute numbers of Twa, the original inhabitants (also known as Batwa), and Swahili-speaking people from Democratic Republic of the Congo and Tanzania also reside in the country.[37] A significant phenomenon from retaining African created borders and polities in Burundi is apparent in the language. Historically, the two ethnic groups that comprised the overwhelming majority of the country both spoke the BaNtu language Rundi (also

---

[37] The Twa are commonly referred to as Pygmies. However, due to the pejorative nature of this designation, we will refrain from calling this ethnic group such. In this book they will be referred to as Twa.

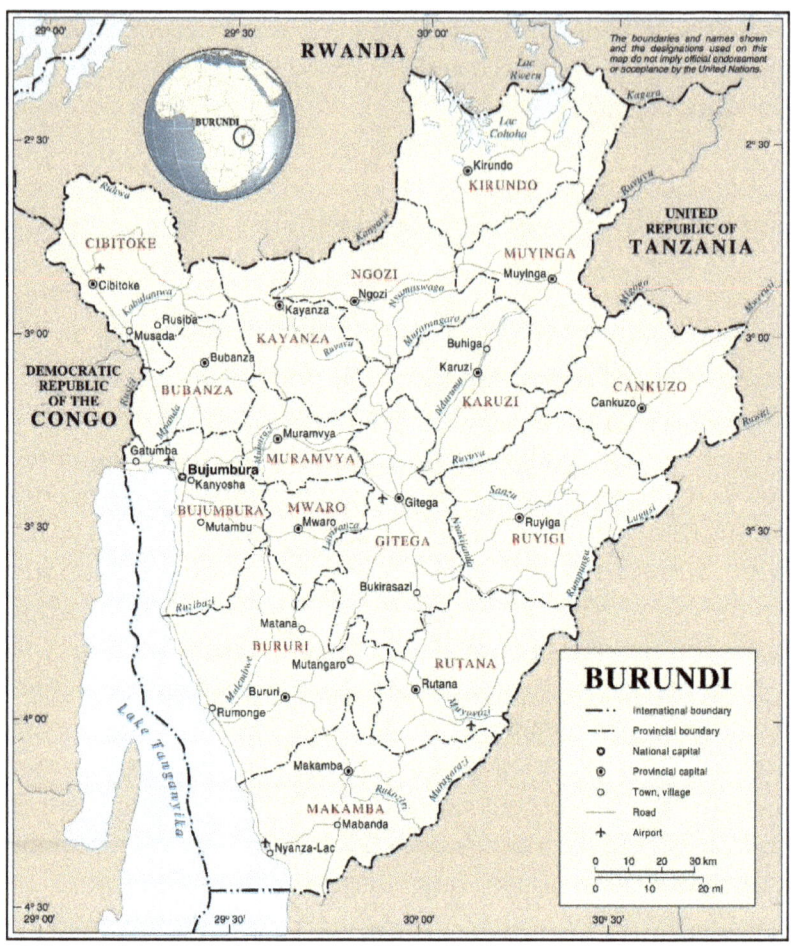

Map 5.3 Contemporary Map of Burundi

Source: United Nations

Map 5.3 portrays the political and traditional boundaries of the Republic of Burundi. Burundi is a rare case where traditional borders were retained during and after the European partition of Africa.

referred to as Kirundi), and presently, Rundi is one of the official languages in the country. Although French is also spoken and Swahili is the language of trade in parts of the country, an extremely large number of people speak Rundi, as their ancestors did, creating an uncommon instance of linguistic homogeneity in an African country south of the Sahara desert.[38]

In Burundi – and other areas in the region – a pastoral-cultivator relationship dominated as a response to drought. Cultivators, during these times of crisis, were not able to provide subsistence for their people for long unpredictable stretches of time. They beseeched the pastoralists for assistance with food since the pastoralists held the only consistent food source – cattle. The general practice of the pastoralists were to not eat their cattle.[39] Rather, they drank the milk, made cheese and butter which sustained them until the end of drought periods. The relationship between the pastoralists and cultivators developed into a ruler-client system with pastoralists as the ruling class and cultivators as the clients or peasant class. Throughout the centuries, Burundi became the terminus for many pastoral and cultivator clans. In the early sixteenth century, the beginning of what would become the Kingdom of Burundi, was founded in the northwest mountains. There, Ntare Karemera, a pastoralist, established the first ruling dynasty in the fifteenth century.[40] Other pastoralist ruling dynasties and clans followed in the coming years.

In the first half of the seventeenth century and the second half of the eighteenth century, drought conditions worsened. As a

---

[38] After the Arab Muslim invasion and conquest of north Africa in the eighth century, Arabic was imposed on the population. Thus, in north Africa, linguistic homogeneity also exists, but it was not African induced.

[39] B.A. Ogot, editor, *Africa from the Sixteenth to the Eighteenth Century*, Vol. 5. *General History of Africa*, abridged edition. (Berkeley: University of California, 1999), 403.

[40] Ibid, 403.

consequence, cultivators were forced to enter relationships with pastoralists for survival. Although similar relationships existed prior to adverse climatic conditions, they became more polarized. Pastoralists created royal lineages based on cattle and their ability to control the activities of the cultivators.[41] It was during this period that the Tutsis' – a pastoralist ethnic group – rule was established and intensified.

The Tutsi Royal Dance

Tutsi culture was designed around their cattle herding practices and principles of royalty were incorporated, creating a virtually inseparable nexus between the two phenomena. As an integral part of the culture, the Tutsis traditionally performed their Intore royal dance – "dance of heroes" in English – to validate and maintain rule. Royal dance and drum groups performed solely for the king during significant ceremonies.[42] Currently, due to the civil strife of the late twentieth century in Burundi and Rwanda, the Tutsi royal dance is seldom performed as a ritual in the open if at all in the region.[43] However,

---

[41] B.A. Ogot, editor, *Africa from the Sixteenth to the Eighteenth Century*, Vol. 5. *General History of Africa*, abridged edition. (Berkeley: University of California, 1999), 403-4. For a more exhaustive discussion on the Burundi-Rwanda-Uganda complex see, D.T. Niane, editor, *African from the Twelfth to the Sixteenth Century*, Vol. 4. *General History of Africa*, abridged edition. (Berkeley: University of California, 1997), 199-208.

[42] I found a rare documentary on YouTube about the Tutsis in Rwanda. It highlights the activities of the royal family and includes an excerpt of the royal dance. See, *A Giant People, Tutsi Monarch Kingdom, Rwanda 1939*. https://www.youtube.com/watch?v=crMFu-86tnI. Accessed July 11, 2019.

[43] At a dance critics national conference (1990), the critics were dismayed by the gross misrepresentations of world dance. They were pleasantly surprised, however, when they saw embedded within one of the videos live footage of the Tutsi royal dance. The movie was MGM's 1950 remake of "King Solomon's Mines." See, https://www.latimes.com/archives/la-xpm-1990-09-05-ca-712-story.html.

contemporary secular renditions are sometimes performed on the concert stage for entertainment.

The Intore dance is traditionally performed by men. It is a lively but simultaneously graceful dance. The torso is held in a high position and is barely moved. Most of the body movements are confined to the legs with complimentary arm movements. Either a spear is held in each hand or a spear in one hand and a shield in the other, and arms are held at a distance from the body. Elbows point towards the sky, or behind the dancer and the arms move towards and away from the body in conjunction with leg raises and other movements. Although the torso does not move, the head may move in circular and whipping motions to accentuate the white "hair" ornament hanging down from the ceremonial head coverings. Movement vocabulary includes jumps with both legs, lunges with one leg and landing on one knee, foot percussive steps, marches, hops backward and forward, and so on.

The attire worn during execution of the Tutsi royal dance is no less striking. The dancers' chests are primarily bare, but dancers sometimes wear white or multicolored sashes crisscrossed on the chest. Elaborately decorated multicolored beaded necklaces are also often worn (see Figure 5.4). On the bottom half of the body, the dancers wear long kilts with a shorter apron overlaid on top cut on a slant. Long strands of raffia or other grassy material hang from the longer side of the apron. The raffia can be natural colored or multicolored. The kilt is primarily red or white – though other colors have been witnessed. The apron is usually white to contrast with the colors of the kilt. In addition to raffia, the apron contains geometric patterns that are woven into it. Bells are usually tied to the ankles to accentuate the foot percussive movements and grace of the dancers. Some Tutsi royal dance performances include copious numbers of drummers. Others include drumming during a portion of the performance, but it ceases during the

Figure 5.3 Intore Dance of Heroes

Figure 5.4 depicts Tutsi royal dancers performing the Intore dance in traditional regalia.

climax of the dance. Last, the Tutsi royal dance may also be performed with no drumming at all utilizing percussive foot movements as both an integral part of the dance and as music for such. Similar to most traditional dances brought to the concert stage, contemporary displays of the Intore on the concert stage exhibit varying degrees of traditional regalia elements. The core of the movement vocabulary is retained, however.

Western Africa

6   Western Africa

While under-researched in the field of history when compared to estern localities, West Africa is perhaps one of the most widely researched regions on the continent of Africa when contrasted with other African regions.[44] In addition to research conducted by scholars in diverse disciplines for the creation of written narratives, people of African descent in the Diaspora are engaged in research that enables them to trace their genetic lineage to the region. The three to five thousand African Americans that have relocated to Accra, Ghana's capital, and the countless numbers of migrations by people from the African Diaspora to Senegal, Nigeria, and other countries in West Africa are the result of such research. Therefore, our study on dance history in Western Africa will highlight a small country often overlooked by researchers, and an ancient phenomenon in the region that is also scarcely researched. Such will facilitate an understanding of the dances and traditions passed down from founding cultures

---

[44] Scholars of the transatlantic slave trade, and African Diaspora culture, conduct copious amounts of research on Nigeria and to a lesser degree, Ghana. Truth be told, there are renditions of the Yoruba religion in most of the Caribbean Islands, the United States, Brazil, Cuba, Haiti, and other locales in the diaspora. Additionally, traditionally dances from Guinea, Mali, and Senegambia are currently popular and is driving much research on the cultures that gave birth to the dances in that region.

Western Africa

Map 6.1 Map of Western Africa

Map 6.1 depicts common landmasses understood to be in West Africa. The borders to the East and Southeast are fluid contingent upon the researcher. For example, for the purposes of this study, Cameroon is considered in West Africa. However, other studies have placed Cameroon under the purview of Central Africa.

The Gambia, Small but Significant

The Gambia is the smallest country in Africa. Its name is taken from the river that runs the length of the entire country through the middle. Located in West Africa, the country borders Senegal on three sides and the Gambia River provides direct access to the Atlantic Ocean. Although presently culturally diverse, the original inhabitants of the country are a mystery. Large monoliths located in The Gambia and in Senegal between the Gambia and Senegal Rivers add more questions rather than answers to the original resident query.

More than one thousand monuments comprising four large groups of stone circles are located in an area slightly over 62 miles (100km) wide and 217.5 miles (350km) long and runs the length of the Gambian River. In addition to the ninety-three stone circles, burial mounds, graves, iron tools, and pottery are witnessed at the site. To date, the earliest of these monuments has been dated at 200 BCE and the latest is dated at the sixteenth century CE, highlighting the fact that this monolith constructing society has maintained its tradition for more than one thousand five hundred years. Although stone circles are found in other locations in the world, nowhere else in the world has there been such a large concentration of stone circles.[45] Coined the Senegambian Stone Circles, the site is on the United Nations Educational Scientific and Cultural Organization's (UNESCO) World Heritage List.

The culture that built these monuments existed within a prosperous, highly organized, complex, and lasting society. A

---

[45] Stone Circles also exist in the Middle East, Europe, Japan, Australia, and other locations around the world.

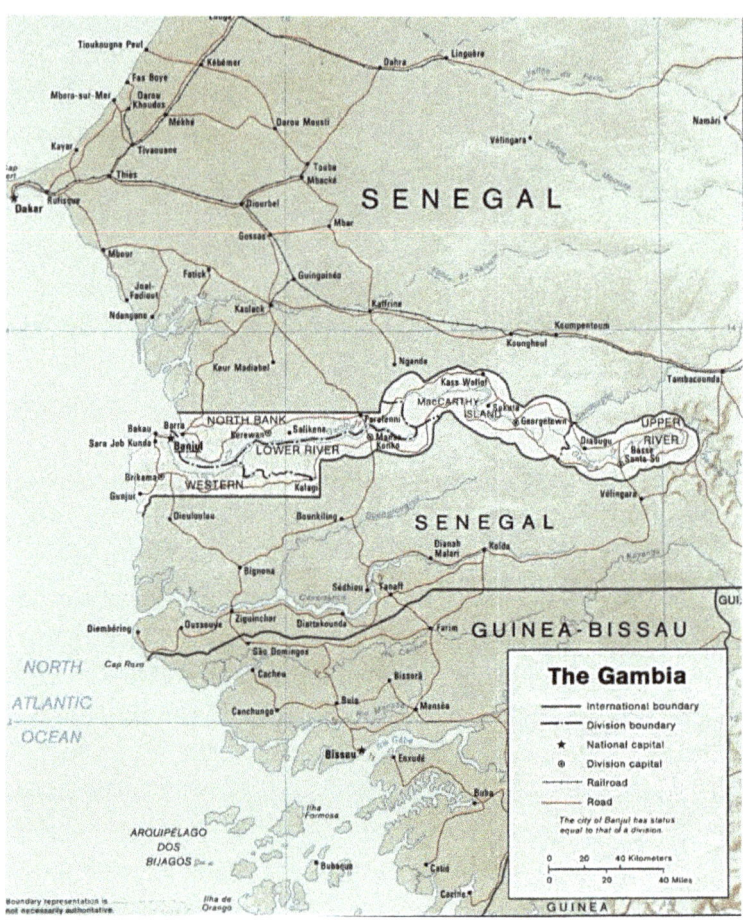

Map 6.2 The Gambia

Map 6.2 depicts The Gambia surrounded by Senegal on three sides. The Gambia is the smallest country on the African continent.

survey of the population in The Gambia reveals diverse ethnic groups residing in the country. However, scholars agree that the Ajamat and the Serer either arrived at or were indigenous to the Senegambian area before the arrival of any of the other ethnic groups. Consequently, scholars believe that the monoliths are a creation of the Ajamat and the Serer ethnic groups. Additionally, it has also been posited that the Ajamat (and their sub-clans) and the Serer may share a common ancestor and therefore are related. For the purposes of our study we will focus on the Ajamat.

Kasa, Dance of the Ajamat

Although the Ajamat can be found in several locations throughout the Senegambia region, particularly Guinea-Bissau, Senegal, and The Gambia, this chapter will emphasize the Ajamat in The Gambia. The Ajamat is popularly known by name "Jola" (also spelled Diola in French) which is of Mandinka origin. However, this ethnic group with its largest concentrations of people in Southern Gambia and Southern Senegal, traditionally refers to themselves as Ajamat.[46] The Ajamat was most resistant to the imposition of foreign religions prior to the late nineteenth century. After which, those that did convert, continued to practice traditional religious systems or elements of such along with Islam. Consequently, the Ajamat possess the largest number of devotees of an African traditional faith within the Senegambian region.[47] Their determination to continue the religious practices of their ancestors is significant

---

[46] The Ajamat is one of many sub-clans belonging to the Jola (Diola, French spelling) ethnic group. The term "Jola" is Wolof in origin. The Ajamat branch of the Jola ethnic group resides in Southern Gambia and Southern Senegal.
[47] Robert M. Baum, *Shrines of the Slave Trade: Diola Religion and Society in Precolonial Senegambia* (New York: Oxford University Press, 1999), 3.

because age-old dance systems are integral components of their spiritual systems.

Historically, the Ajamat established egalitarian non-centralized societies. Decisions were reached through majority consent and elders served as mediators during any disputes. There were no government officials, kings, slaves, or other class determinants.[48]

The Ajamat have historically been and many currently still are expert rice harvesters. Despite the appearance of abundant vegetation in the areas where they traditionally inhabited, drought was a familiar occurrence. Thus, dance systems were developed to navigate the uncertainty of rice farming. Such dances encourage increased rainfall, an abundant yield, and they display gratitude via the harvest celebration dance festivals.

Kasa is a celebration dance traditionally performed to celebrate an abundant rice harvest.[49] Although dance troupes will perform a portion of Kasa's steps in unison currently, it was historically performed as a solo. A circle would be formed from the standing arrangements of the drummers and the spectator-dancers. A person would emerge from among the spectators, to perform Kasa dance movements in the center of the circle. Afterwards, the dancer would return to their original space among the crowd and another spectator would appear to dance in the center of the circle, hence the term 'spectator-dancer.'[50] Everyone in the village participates. The tradition of village participation is apparent in contemporary performances of Kasa. Often, the audience is asked to come on stage and dance.

---

[48] See Robert M. Baum, *Shrines of the Slave Trade: Diola Religion and Society in Precolonial Senegambia* (New York: Oxford University Press, 1999).

[49] Kasa is known as Ekonkon to Ajamat in Casamance, Southern Senegal. It was traditionally performed for the same purpose, rice harvest celebration. Presently, Kasa/Ekonkon is also performed for other non-agricultural celebrations.

[50] See Ofosuwa M. Abiola, *History Dances: Chronicling the History of Traditional Mandinka Dance* (London: Routledge, 2019).

Western Africa 77

Figure 6.1 Kasa, Corichow Dance Troupe, The Gambia, 2004

Photograph: Ofosuwa M. Abiola

Figure 6.1 depicts Moundaw Tamba (right), a member of Corichow Dance Troupe, teaching an audience member, Monica, the dance Kasa during a performance in The Gambia.

Figure 6.2 Gambian National Dance and Music Troupe, USA, 1998

Photograph: Ofosuwa M. Abiola

Figure 6.2 portrays a dancer in the Gambian National Dance and Music Troupe playing clackers (right) while other members perform acrobats.

Kasa employs a noticeably acute torso in the low and medium positions (see Figure 6.1). The arms move in a circular motion and opposite the legs. Thus, when the leg is raised the arms are in a low position and vice versa. Each leg is raised with the knee bent and is thrust to the ground with a hop produced by both feet. With the exception of holding the torso at a constant acute angle, there are virtually no upper body movements in Kasa. Last, the spectator-dancers play clackers when the soloist enters the circle to perform. Clackers are narrow blocks of wood that are sometimes shaped narrower at the ends. The clackers are played with constant syncopated rhythms in-between each pause.

The traditional instruments played for Kasa performances are Kutiro drums. Kutiros are fashioned in different sizes and are played with a stick-and-hand technique. They are constructed from a single block of wood, are wider at the top and are secured on to the musician by a strap around the shoulder. The top of the drum is constructed from goat or antelope skin and is held on by pegs and laces.

Traditionally, Ajamat men and women in The Gambia wore raffia or other types of grass-like skirts or kilts while performing Kasa. Copious strands of beads were warn around the waist and crisscrossed in the front and back from the shoulders to the waist. Short grass ankle, neck, and wrist ornaments were also worn. Cowrie shells were worn to decorate and accentuate the flow of the grass garments.

Figure 6.3 The Kutiro Drum, 1978

Photograph: Michael Huet

Figure 6.3 depicts an Ajamat drummer in Casamance (Southern Senegal) playing the kutiro.

The Fulani of West Africa

Most ethnic groups that reside in specific countries in Africa today migrated to their present location at some time in the past or in some cases, very recently. History notwithstanding, ethnic groups are generally associated with the country they reside in currently. Thus, the Yoruba in Nigeria, the Akan in Ghana, and the Dogon in Mali are all considered to be in their native countries. However, one ethnic group defies these generalizations. The Fulani, also known as Fulbe, Fula, Halpulaar, Peul, among other names, are one of the largest ethnic groups in West Africa and is the largest nomadic group in the world. Their language, Pular, belongs to the Niger-Congo language group. They are located throughout the continent of Africa from Senegal, West Africa to Sudan, East Africa, and from the Atlantic Ocean to the Red Sea. However, they exist in greatest numbers in West Africa. Although the Fulani are the largest nomadic ethnic group in the world, it does not preclude the existence of sedentary factions among them. To date, many Fulani reside in urban and metropolitan centers and though they are collectively one of the majority groups in West Africa, the Fulani are minorities in many of the non-west African countries where they traded their nomadic lifestyles for sedentary ones.[51] Historically, the Fulani that retained their pastoral nomadic lifestyles were referred to as Mbororo. A modern-day example of a traditional Mbororo group is the Wodaabe. Globalization, drought, urbanization of traditional grazing lands, among other things, have forced some Fulani groups to adapt to semi-nomadic existences, however, they may still be preferred to be

---

[51] The Fulani are minorities in many countries outside of West Africa where they reside currently. By contrast, they form a majority in Guinea and Guinea-Bissau, and they are the second largest ethnic group in The Gambia and Senegal.

referred to as Mbororo though they are not fully nomadic.⁵²
Both sedentary and nomadic Fulani also refer to themselves as
Fulbe.

Historically, the overwhelming majority of Fulani were
pastoralists that moved from terrain to terrain with their herd
seeking green pasture for their cattle to consume. Their cattle
provided milk, cheese, butter, and sustenance when other
sources of food were unavailable. Accordingly, they bonded
with their herd, named each cow, and formed social and
spiritual institutions around their cattle. Subsequently, wealth in
Fulani social systems was determined by the number of cows
owned. However, status was connected to lifestyle. Fully
nomadic Fulani were – and still are – admired. The code of
values that dictates proper Fulani behavior and decorum is
known as *Pulaku* which is taught to Fulani from an early age
and validated during the rite of passage process.⁵³

The antiquity of Fulani pastoral cultural system has been
substantiated by scholars. Rock art dated at least to 300 BCE was
recovered in Tassili n'Ajjer, Southern Algeria, that
archaeologists attribute to the Fulani and other current pastoral
societies in North and West Africa. Certain rock paintings
among the Tassili n'Ajjer collection exhibit proto-Fulani cultural
tenets. Historian Amadou Hampaté Bâ, Fulani cultural
specialist, identified depictions of the Fulani Lotori ceremony –
an ox origin celebration – among two thousand three hundred
year old rock art.⁵⁴

---

⁵² For an example of a modern-day semi-nomadic Fulani group that refers to themselves as Mbororo see, Henri Bocquene, *Memoirs of a Mbororo: The Life of Ndudi Umaru: Fulani Nomad of Cameroon* (New York: Berghahn Books, 2002). To the Fulani, fully nomadic lifestyles confers status.
⁵³ For a modern-day example of how Pulaku operates in everyday Fulani life, see, Bocquene, *Memoirs of a Mbororo*, 72.
⁵⁴ See, Department of the Arts of Africa, Oceania, and the Americas. "The Fulani/Fulbe People." *Heilbrunn Timeline of Art History*. New York: The Metropolitan Museum of Art, 2000.

Yoleli and the Fulani

The traditional dance Yoleli has myriad functions in Fulani society.[55] Also referred to as Fula Fare – dance of the Fula – in Susu, Yoleli is performed as part of the naming ceremony ritual or the "dennaboo." The naming ceremony occurs on the seventh day of the newborn's life.[56] For nomadic Fulani, the dance, along with its songs and drum rhythms, are also performed to facilitate the gathering of the herd. Last, the dance is performed at weddings and other celebrations as well.

Yoleli, coined the calabash dance by non-Fulani spectators, was traditionally performed to rhythms played on the tummude or calabash. The tummude is comprised of a large calabash cut in half played across the chest or on the floor with the hollow side facing down. However, the floor technique was used less often than the chest. The dance is executed to a moderate to fast tempo. The movement vocabulary heavily employs the lower half of the body and accompanying arm movements. Head movements are not traditionally a component of the dance. The root step is executed by a skipping motion with one foot while the other foot is hopped behind it.[57] Alternately, the motion is repeated on the other side of the body. The arms are held high at the shoulder level, elbows pointing downward. They are intermittently positioned close to the body when a leg is placed

---

[55] Yoleli is the traditional Fulani name for the dance, however the Susu and the Mandinka refer to the dance as Fula Fare, "Fulani dance."

[56] The day of the naming ceremony is not static. Some Mbororo perform the naming ceremony on the eighth day. Weather and social occurrences may also influence the timing of the ceremony. See, Henri Bocquene, *Memoirs of a Mbororo: The Life of Ndudi Umaru: Fulani Nomad of Cameroon* (New York: Berghahn Books, 2002), 72.

[57] The root step is a movement that retains the original core that comprised the dance step at its inception in antiquity. For more on root steps see, Ofosuwa M. Abiola, *History Dances: Chronicling the History of Traditional Mandinka Dance* (London: Routledge, 2019), 44.

82 Western Africa

Figure 6.4 Fulani Dancer, Guinea, 1978

Photograph: Michael Huet

Figure 6.4 depicts a Fulani dancer performing acrobats in the dance Yoleli. Notice he is also playing a tummude (calabash drum).

behind the other, and away from the body when a skip is executed. Yoleli also employs abrupt squats with equally abrupt recovery to a standing position directly before or after performing the skip hop step. The torso is acute, held in the high position for some steps, and the medium for others.

The attire of the Fulani during dance performances varies with the conditions of their lifestyles and the materials in the regions where they reside or traverse. Mbororo Womens' garments virtually always include a type of wrapped skirt fashioned from weaved cloth and a matching short-sleeved blouse. Layers of wrapped fabric are added depending on region and lifestyle. The amount of fabric used for wrapping and where the wrapped textiles are employed also varies. For example, Fulani women may wear a piece of fabric on their head. Alternatively, they may wear several layers of wrapped fabric on their heads giving the appearance of the person as several inches taller in height. They may also wrap the fabric around the body. "Town" Fulani will incorporate elements of Fulani attire with the traditional dress of the location, or they may dress entirely identical to the residents of the area.

Perhaps the most distinctive elements of traditional female Fulani dress are their traditional jewelry, hairstyles, and their facial tattoos. Large gold Fulani twist earrings, decorative black facial tattoos and elaborate braided hairstyles with amber ornaments have virtually become the signposts of Fulani tradition. However, the utilization of these items is contingent upon fully nomadic, semi-nomadic, and sedentary lifestyles, as well as the region in Africa.

Male's garments during dance executions are equally as diverse and is also contingent upon the type of Fulani, Mbororo, semi-nomadic, or "town" Fulani and on the region. Generally, many Fulani men traditionally wear tunics and pants, however the length, embroidery, and extravagance of the tunics and the type of pants worn widely vary. Some Fulani men also wear fabric wrapped around their faces. It should be noted that the Fulani converted to Islam in the second millennium, far earlier than many other African ethnic groups. Thus, Islamic tenets influence much of the ceremonial and secular dress. Though, there are exceptions to this rule. Those Fulani that retained their full nomadic lifestyles generally did not convert to Islam.[58] Moreover, many that did convert to Islam continued to practice their traditional African religious systems alongside Islam, or they Africanized it. That is, they incorporated African religious tenets in with Islamic practices.

---

[58] The sect of Fulani known as Wodaabe have retained their full nomadic lifestyles. Subsequently, the Wodaabe continue to practice the religious traditions of their ancestors. Their attire is also indicative of traditional non-Islamic dress.

Central Africa

7 Central Africa

The location of the equator virtually splits the African continent generally, and Central Africa particularly, in half. Thus, Central Africa is one of the most foliage prolific regions on the continent. Yet, because of its location in the center of the continent and its northern and southern environs, Central Africa is simultaneously exceedingly diverse. The region includes the enormous countries of Chad and the Democratic Republic of the Congo, and the smaller and more centralized Central African Republic.[59] As a consequence of location and placement of the equator, deserts, rainforests, and grassland savannas can all be witnessed in Central Africa. It is equally rich in ancient artifacts, as the cave engravings of Kiantapo and Kiamakonde illustrate. The name conferred on the cave, *Kiantapo*, "the place where there are tattoos" in the Kiluba language, succinctly portrays the aesthetic of the caves' engravings.[60] Created from

---

[59] This discussion on Central Africa will solely include the countries that are directly in the center of the continent of Africa. Thus, countries considered central east or central west will not be discussed here. Instead, such territories may be discussed in sections of the book covering East or West Africa respectively.

[60] The Kiantapo and the Kiamakonde cave engravings are located in the Democratic Republic of the Congo in Central Africa. They are classified as rock art and are not as well-known as the rock art of Southern Africa or the Tassili n'Ajjer rock art in Southern Algeria. For a discussion on the Democratic Republic of the Congo cave engravings and other rock art in the

Central Africa

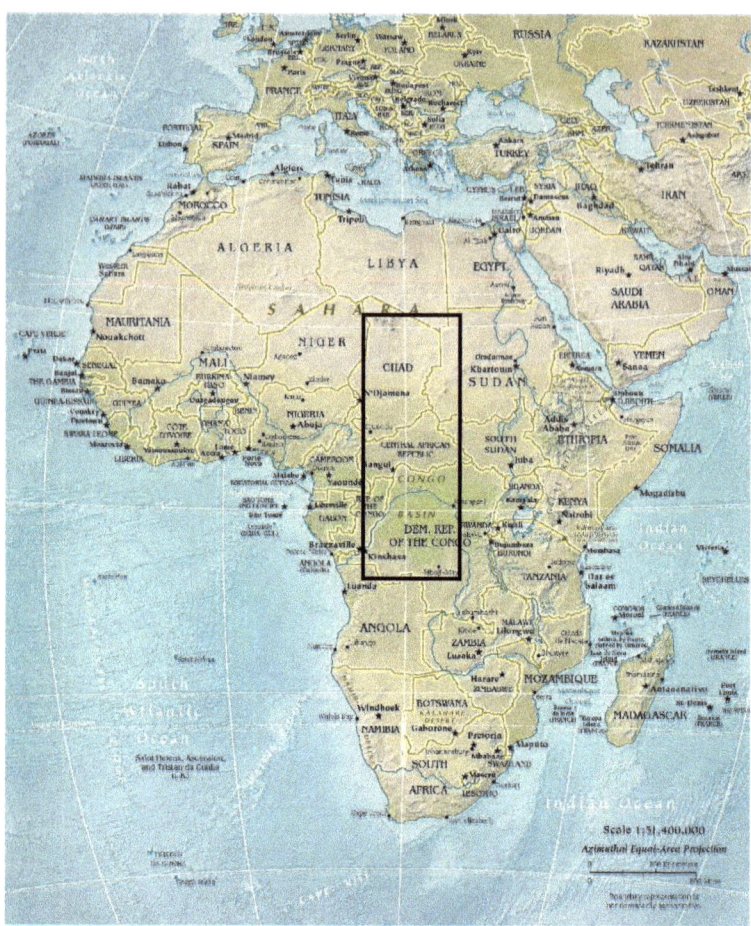

Map 7.1 Central Africa

Map 7.1 illustrates the area of the African continent that this study considers Central Africa.

Central African region and other parts of Africa see, Jean-Löic Le Quellec, *Rock Art in Africa: Mythology and Legend*. Translated by Paul Bahn, (Paris: Editions Flammarion, 2004).

Figure 7.1 Kiantapo Cave Engravings, Democratic Republic of the Congo

Photograph: Ofosuwa M. Abiola

endless indentations or holes of diverse sizes, and an abundance of geometric lines and shapes, depictions of mammals, birds, snakes and fish are apparent. Currently, Central Africa is also the location of some of the earth's most precious and most controversial minerals including coltan, gold, and diamonds.

Chad

Chad is situated in the center of Africa, north of the Central African Republic. Its location is reminiscent of the telephone switchboards of the late nineteenth to mid-twentieth centuries, because of its importance to its border countries in North, Central, East, and West Africa. The constant swelling and waning of Lake Chad through millennia pulled people to the lake region from various territories on the outskirts of the lake. To date, Lake Chad provides water to over thirty million people in the countries of Cameroon, Chad, Niger, and Nigeria. The constant adjusting of diverse populations as a response to Lake Chad's incessant increases and decreases, create a backdrop from which to study the culture and dances of the country.

Chad has been posited as one of the potential sites of human origin due to the discovery of a six to seven million-year-old hominid like skull, Sahelanthropus Tchadensis. Evidence of human settlement dates to at least 8,000 BCE, and by 7,000 BCE human settlement was permanent. In roughly 5000 BCE pastoralism became the dominant means of production. The earliest Trans-Saharan route was established through Chad after 3,000 BCE. The period also witnessed the rise of the Sao people who are known for the fortified walled cities they built. Chad is also the location of other powerful ancient and medieval empires such as Zanghawa and Kanem Bornu. In the southern regions of the country, iron smelting techniques were known and practiced as early as 540 BCE. Presently, the Sara is the largest ethnic group in Chad and is comprised of several sub-groups. The Mbaye is one such ethnic group.

Chad, Mbaye, and the Klag

The Klag is performed for celebrations by the Mbaye that reside in Southern regions of Chad. The Mbaye is also known as Mbai, Moissala, Sara Mbai, among other names. Among all the dances performed by the Mbaye, the Klag is the most popular in the region. Although it is performed with an acute torso depending on the practitioner, Klag is also performed with the torso erect.

Both knees are bent and the feet alternate with one stomp each or they stomp twice before switching to the other. In Klag, rapid torso contractions are emphasized. The arms are held away from the body with the elbows pointing towards the back. For women, pelvic contractions are incorporated in the movement vocabulary as well, but more as an extension of executing the torso contraction movements. Some men, however, employ pelvic contractions along with the torso contractions as a regular component of the dance. There are no kicks in the traditional movement vocabulary of this historic Chadian dance. Squats and recovery, shuffles, hops, and leaps are also not traditionally displayed in Klag.

In addition to syncopated clapping and singing or chanting, several musicians play traditional drums, or the tam tams. One type of tam tam is tall easily reaching the chest of its male drummer, the gangué. It is constructed from a long narrow hollow log and uncovered on the bottom with a whole carved out to facilitate resonation. The top contains a skin fastened by large pegs wedged around the body of the drum. It is played by standing drummers with a hand technique. The smaller tam tams are covered by a skin on the top fastened by rope that is tied and interlocked with the rope from the top and the bottom, or it is fastened by pegs in the same fashion as the large tam tams (see Figure 7.2).

Traditional dress includes a long multicolored wrapped skirt worn by the women. Numerous strands of beads hanging from the shoulders are warn crisscrossed in the front and back and hangs loosely over the copious amounts of beads worn on the waist. The men wear kilts that vary in length and can be any length from below the knees to the ankles. White raffia or grass anklets are warn on the ankles or the bottom end of the calves just above the ankles. Bead strands crisscrossed in the front and back are also worn by the men. They also wear beaded or textile arm bands on the upper part of the arms just after the shoulders.

Figure 7.2 Mbaye Orchestra, Chad, 1978

Photograph: Michael Huet

Figure 7.2 portrays musicians in a typical Mbaye drum orchestra. The tall hand beaten tam tam on the right is the gangué.

Currently, Mbaye that reside in cities and towns wear clothing contemporaneous with their African counterparts across the continent. Thus, women wear wrapped skirts, matching, tops and a head wrap. Men often wear tunics and matching pants made from African fabric, or Western clothes such as jeans and tee-shirts. Nonetheless, when occasions arise that call for celebrating, it is not uncommon to witness men retrieving their tam tams to play for the occasion, and both men and women performing the Klag.

The Democratic Republic of the Congo

The Democratic Republic of the Congo is also referred to as Congo-Kinshasa.[61] Congo-Kinshasa, in addition to sharing a border with The Republic of the Congo or Congo-Brazzaville (and several other countries), is centrally located in Africa and shares a large border to the south with Angola. Although these are three separate countries presently, before and during the slave trade this was a massive territory where ethnic groups and nations shared similar cultural tenets. As discussed earlier, scholars have identified one common root language that the seemingly countless ethnicities and nations in this central African region have originated from, BaNtu.[62] Moreover, roughly forty to forty-five percent of all enslaved Africans transported to the Americas – North, South, and Central America, and the islands in-between – were shipped from this location in Central Africa.

The foundations for kingdoms and other societal structures were organized in antiquity, and by the fourteenth century, the peoples of The Democratic Republic of the Congo established prosperous kingdoms based on farming and trade. Their societies were built on royal lineages that legitimized their authority through religion. In Congo-Kinshasa, the Luba and the Lunda were responsible for founding the dominant kingdoms in the area.

---

[61] Two countries in central Africa contain the name 'Congo,' the Democratic Republic of the Congo – the capital is Kinshasa – and the Republic of the Congo – the capital is Brazzaville. To avoid confusion, scholars often refer to the countries by attaching their capitals to the name 'Congo' separated by a hyphen. Thus, the two countries are known as Congo-Kinshasa and Congo-Brazzaville respectively.

[62] Bantu-speaking people migrated from West Africa and have spread to Central, West Central, East, and South Africa. See Kevin Shillington, *History of Africa* (New York: Palgrave Macmillan, 2012), 59-60.

94 Central Africa

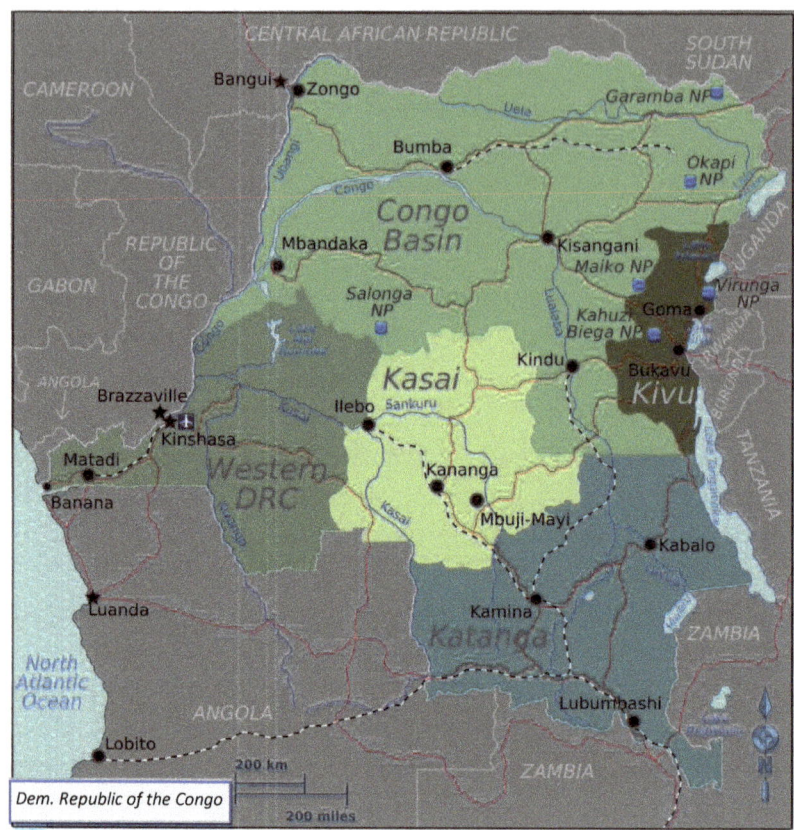

Map 7.2 Democratic Republic of the Congo

Source: Perry-Casteneda Library Map Collection

Map 7.2 depicts the political borders of the country the Democratic Republic of the Congo. In addition to its abundance of rich minerals, and precious stones, such as diamonds among others, it contains a hefty supply of coltan. Tantalum capacitors are produced via coltan and is used in many electronic devices including mobile phones.

The Mwaash Mbooy: A Bushong Royal Dance

The Kuba is comprised of several ethnic groups with similar cultural, religious, economic and social systems. The Kuba became a united nation of people in the seventeenth century. It was located between the Kasai and the Sankuru Rivers (see Map 7.2) in the Democratic Republic of the Congo, and the predominant group within the Kuba was the Bushong. Many of the nations that comprise the Kuba state originated in Mongo country located north of the Sankuru River. The southward migrations lasted well into the mid-twentieth century but commenced roughly four hundred years ago. Prior to Kuba migrations into the region, it was not without indigenous peoples. As such, the Mbuti, Baka, Batwa, and Kete peoples resided there before the Kuba's arrival. This rich territory consisted of equatorial forest, rich savanna, a number of intersecting rivers, and a host of natural resources.

History is very important to the Kuba. The king is the primary custodian of the dynasty's genealogy, followed by the *bulaam*, his eldest son, and a handful of trusted unrelated historians that must also thoroughly learn the genealogical delineation of the dynasty.

The Mwaash Mbooy is a Bushong masked dance performed for the royal court.[63] Within the genre of royal dances, the Mwaash Mbooy has the most elaborate attire and mask. It is a full body mask dance where the dancer is covered from head to toe with copious amounts of beads, cowrie shells, textiles, feathers, and raffia grass. The Mwaash Mbooy mask is kept in the king's possession and lent to the dancer during the ceremonial inauguration of the masks, a long ceremony involving many royal mask dancers. Each mask worn by the

---

[63] It should not be misconstrued that court in this sense is connected to any legal processes. The royal court refers to locations where kings, queens, and any other royalty assemble to be addressed.

Figure 7.3 Mwaash Mbooy Masked Dancer, Congo-Kinshasa, 1978

Photograph: Michael Huet

Figure 7.3 depicts the full regalia of a Mwaash Mbooy dancer. The Mwaash Mbooy mask is only one of many masks each with their own name and meaning.

dancer possesses its own name. The Mwaash Mbooy mask dance is significant in royal rituals. It symbolizes and validates the spiritual nature of the king and sets him apart from the mundane. It also represents Woot, the founder of Kuba. During the Mwaash Mbooy ceremony, the mask arrives after the ceremony has already begun and emerges from the forest. The Ngady Mwaash mask is the sister of Woot. The presence of this mask facilitates balance. The sky god is depicted by the MBoom mask. Bird masks also dance in the royal ceremony to protect the area from evil while simultaneously entertaining the spectators. Generally the ceremonial inauguration of the masks is attended by everyone in the village. However, spectators are not permitted to witness all royal masks. Some are danced solely for the royal court and are sometimes not seen for decades at a time.

Unmasked dancers in the ceremonial inauguration of the masks perform dance movements around the masked dancers. Movement vocabulary for the unmasked dancers include subtle foot and arm movements. Shoulders move up and down in sync with the arm movements. Dancers hold leaves, canes, feathers, among other props. Torso is held in diverse position depending on the step and is upright to acute in the high position. Turns are employed and knees are lifted and placed back on the ground to the rhythm.

Space does not permit an extensive description of the dance attire, but as a starting point, Kuba cloth, fashioned from raffia palm, is profusely utilized for dance attire for the unmasked (and masked) dancers.[64] The length varies and depends upon the status or position of the dancer. The royal guardians wear knee-

---

[64] See Michael Huet, *The Dances of Africa* (New York: Harry N. Abrams, Inc., Publishers, 1994), 154, for a brief discussion on the Kuba. Also see Michael Huet, *The Dance, Art and Ritual of Africa* (New York: Pantheon Book, 1978), 193-4, and plates 244-46, for a discussion on Mwaash Mbooy masks and rituals, and photographs.

length prolifically pleated skirts made of colorfully weaved Kuba cloth. The chests are bare, accenting the layers of neck adornments made of cowrie shells, gourds, and beads, among other things. The skirts also contain a top layer of pleated Kuba cloth and the head is adorned with cowrie shell and beaded and Kuba cloth hats. The cowrie shells on the head pieces are sewn on in decorative patterns and they are so abundant that only small sections of the cloth on the hat is visible.

The drums played for the royal ceremony are carved from a single log of long narrow timber. The skin on the head is sewn on via cord stitched through small holes in a band of leather that extends onto the rim just beneath the top opening of the drum. The band of leather is then fastened by numerous small wooden pegs around the drum.

8 Conclusion

> *The usual dance was proposed. A large bonfire was made in the yard, and a circle formed by women and children. A female drummer soon made her appearance, and a tam-tam struck their national dance, accompanied with song. Each one by turns stepped out and danced according to their nation.*[65]
>
> - *Theophilus Conneau, 1853*

The impact that the paucity of research on African dance history has on myriad fields cannot be overstated. Embedded within the dances of Africa are repositories of historical narratives, invaluable insights on the mindset of ancient and contemporary peoples, and revelations and budding hints of developing cultural phenomena. Such information greatly contributes to and facilitates deeper understanding in the disciplines of African history, African studies, world history, archaeology and anthropology, pre-colonial studies, women's studies, dance history, world dance, theatre studies, among other fields. It is not enough to uncover previously unknown artifacts if their meaning continues to be a mystery. Indeed, African dance

---

[65] Theophilus, Conneau, *A Slaver's Log Book or 20 Years' Residence in Africa: The Original 1853 Manuscript* (Eaglewood Cliffs: Prentice-Hall, Inc., 1976), 53.

history has much to convey, thus it must be engaged as more than mere entertainment.

Whether studying the millennia-old rock engravings in South Africa or the Democratic Republic of the Congo, or conducting research on the colossal number of ancient monoliths in Senegal and The Gambia, the cultural dances performed today in the regions under study provides indispensable information on the ancient cultures that gave birth to the dances. The purpose and meaning of the dances and by extension the culture and its history are housed in the steps, nuances, and body movements displayed each time the dance is performed. Yet, a potential crisis is imminent. To date, many traditional African dances have fallen into disuse taking with them priceless information. Scholars must undertake the task of engaging the dance systems that are still practiced to avert the future loss of cultural jewels. Last, although this book focusses on history and theory, dance practitioners must become scholars, and scholars must dance to facilitate an accurate understanding of the dance systems, their cultural histories, and the informative bodily nuances that are inaccessible to the nonpractitioner.

Appendix
Table of African Dances

Appendix A lists traditional African dances from various parts of the continent. The ten dances discussed earlier will not be included in the list. The list is intended to add to the body of knowledge of African dances.

A hefty amount of the dances in the table are still practiced currently. However, many are either at risk of extinction or have already fallen into disuse. The information in the Table of Dances derives from the sources below. The omission of dances from many popularly known regions is deliberate. The Table of Dances is meant to expose readers to new information. All the dances listed in the table do not contain full descriptions, the table reflects the most available information that could be substantiated at the time of this writing. Consequently, the Table of Dances is by no means complete. Its purpose is to provide a push for the reader to conduct further research on the dances of Africa.

Sources

Interviews

Yarro Bari
Moundaw Tamba

Moustahpa Bangoura
Omar Bunhatap Jammeh

DVD/Video

Bangoura, Moustapha. *Tinkanyi 1*. DVD. Produced by Marc Sandrolini of Quietcity Productions, 2004.

Bangoura, Moustapha. *Tinkanyi 2*. DVD. Produced by Marc Sandrolini of Quietcity Productions, 2004.

Koumbassa, Youssouf. *Let's Go Wangai 1: Dances from Guinea West Africa*. DVD. B-rave Studio Production, 1999.

Koumbassa, Youssouf. *Let's Go Wangai 2: Dances from Guinea West Africa*. DVD. B-rave Studio Production, 1999.

Books

Akombo, David. *The Unity of Music and Dance in World Cultures.* Jefferson: McFarland & Company, Inc., 2016.

Beaman, Patricia. *World Dance Cultures: From Ritual to Spectacle*. London: Routledge, 2018.

Dagan, Ester A., ed., *The Spirit's Dance in Africa: Evolution, Transformation and Continuity in Sub-Sahara.* Quebec: Galerie Amrad African Arts Publications, 1997.

Huet, Michael. *The Dances of Africa*. Harry N. Abrams, Inc., Publishers, 1994.

Nii-Yartey, Francis. *African Dance in Ghana: Contemporary Transformations*. London: Mot Juste Limited, 2012.

Spencer, Paul, editor. *Society and the Dance: The Social Anthropology of Process and Performance*. London: Cambridge University Press, 2003.

Appendix A Table of African Dances

Dance	Description	Source
Kumpo	Buluff clan of the Jola ethnic group. Originated with the Bainuukas, the dance represents the use of magic to cast out evil doers (The Gambia)	Bari
Domba Yeri Yeriso	Susu dance. At the end of the rainy season, the people come together to celebrate the first taste of the newly harvested cereal (The Gambia)	Bari
Kasa	Jola dance performed by the Casa subclan. After a hard day's work in the rice fields, Kasa is performed (The Gambia, Senegal)	Tamba
Bwola	Acholi royal dance performed to celebrate the installation of a chief (Uganda)	Dagan
Kassa	Mandinka dance performed to encourage the farmers to work hard (Guinea)	Bangoura
Larakaraka	Performed by the Acholi and the Gulu to expose young women to prospective male suitors (Uganda)	Dagan
Sofa	Mandinka hunting dance (Guinea)	Koumbassa

Jondon	Mandinka dance performed by slaves who have been recently acquired (Guinea, Mali)	Tamba
Wolosodon,	Mandinka dance performed by slaves who have been absorbed into the master's family (Guinea, Mali)	Tamba
Jamba Dongo	Mandinka dance. Initiated girls celebrate womanhood (The Gambia)	Tamba
Konkoba	Mande farming dance (Guinea)	Bangoura
Sinte	Landonma, Nalo, and Boffa ethnic groups. Sinte is performed before the rite of passage (Guinea)	Bangoura
Sarki	A Boorana male's wedding dance (Kenya)	Dagan
Yankadi	Danced by the Susu, Temine, and Mendenyi ethnic groups. It is a dance of courtship (Guinea, Sierra Leone)	Bangoura
Molimo	Mbuti dance of the honeybee performed during the honey season (Democratic Republic of the Congo)	Akombo
Macru	Danced by the Susu, Temine, and Mendenyi ethnic groups. Performed as a celebration of the success	Bangoura

	of the courtship (Guinea, Sierra Leone)	
Kulu Dongo	Sarahule healing dance (The Gambia)	Barri
Teminks	Manojo dance that symbolizes worship and is done for war (The Gambia)	Tamba
Tarrienha Ibuga	Bosaga dance performed for general entertainment at celebrations (Uganda)	Dagan
Pilong	Girls rite of passage dance (The Gambia)	Jammeh
Naleyo	Karimojong courtship dance (Uganda)	Dagan
Kuku	Mande dance. Performed for celebrations (Guinea)	Koumbassa
Lamban Jeli/Jali Don	Mandinka. Dance of the jali/jeli (Guinea)	Koumbassa
Domba	Venda premarital dance (South Africa)	Spensor
Sinte	Performed by the Landonma, Baga, and Nalo ethnic groups for rite of passage (Guinea)	Bangoura
Soko	Mandinka preinitiation dance (Guinea)	Bangoura
Jole (Djole, French spelling)	Temine, Susu, and Mandenyi perform mask dance to showcase different masks and their meanings (Sierra Leone, Guinea)	Bangoura
Gomba	Male initiation dance (Mali)	Tiérou
Blin-doo	Male's mask initiation dance (Ivory Coast)	Tiérou

Gnenon	Elder women's dance (Togo)	Tiérou
Malicondi	A territorial dance (Togo)	Tiérou
Sorsorner	From the Baga ethnic group, a rite of passage dance (Guinea)	Koumbassa
Soli Rapide	Mandinka male rite of passage dance (Guinea)	Bangoura
Triba	Baga celebration dance (Guinea)	Koumbassa
Mane	Susu women's dance performed to present skill and beauty of the dance (Guinea)	Bangoura
Yoleli	Fulani name changing dance (the nomadi Fulani are spread across the Sahel region of Africa from West to East)	Bangoura
Guinea Fare	Susu woman's celebration dance (Guinea)	Koumbassa
Dundunba-Konde	Mandinka dance performed to display strength (Guinea)	Koumbassa
Afindrafindrao	A Merina courtship dance performed at the beginning of celebrations (Madagascar)	Dagan
Sofora	Jola. The dance is performed to unify all the clans of the Jola (The Gambia)	Bari
Daka	The Tandroy perform this dance for weddings and ritualistic ceremonies (Madagascar)	Dagan
Mampa Para	Susu rite of passage dance. Its performance includes fire	Bari

	eating, stilt dancing, and acrobatics (The Gambia)	
Komofoli	Bamana initiation dance. Circle dance performed by men and women, and diverse age sets (Mali)	Dagan
Manjani	Mandinka girl's rite of passage dance (Guinea, The Gambia, Senegal)	Jammeh
Kankouran	Mandinka full body mask dance performed to protect the initiates (Guinea, Senegal)	De Jong
Jambadong	Festive Mandinka dance performed to mark the initiate graduate's reentry into society (Southern Senegal, Guinea)	De Jong
Yamama	Mandinka masked dance performed to fight evil spirits (Guinea)	Bangoura
Solindingo	Mande girl's masquerade rite of passage dance honoring Sogolon, Sunjata's mother (Wuli, The Gambia)	Weil
Asafo	Fante warrior dance (Ghana)	Nii-Yartey
Tusya	Samo wedding dance (Burkina Faso)	Dagan
Kurukupaa	Mande elder women's divination masked dance (Wuli, The Gambia)	Weil
Sontokuhoo	Mande girl's rite of passage masquerade dance (The Gambia)	Weil

Senko	Men's masked dance central to girl's first premarital initiation ceremony (The Gambia)	Weil
Egungun	Yoruba ancestor dance (Nigeria)	Beaman
Embaga	Baganda wedding dance (Uganda)	Dagan

About the Author

Dr. Ofosuwa M. Abiola received her Ph.D. in African History. Currently, she is Assistant Professor of Dance History, Coordinator of the Dance Program, and Coordinator of the Honors Program in the Department of Theatre Arts at Howard University. Dr. Abiola is the author of *History Dances: Chronicling the History of Traditional Mandinka Dance,* and the Editor-in-Chief of the peer-reviewed digital journal, *Evoke: A Historical, Theoretical, and Cultural Analysis of Africana Dance and Theatre.* Dr. Abiola is featured as a Master Teacher in the book, *In Good Keeping: Virginia's Folklife Apprenticeships.* She founded, and currently serves as Artistic Director of the *Nankama African Dance Conference.* Dr. Abiola also founded and served as Artistic Director for the traditional African dance company, *Suwabi African Ballet,* for 15 Years. She performed with the company as well. Dr. Abiola apprenticed and performed with Corichow Dance Troupe in The Gambia, West Africa.

Bibliography

Interviews

Master Dancer: Moustapha Bangoura, USA, 2015
Jali/Griot: Ibrahima Camara, Senegal, 2014
Master Dancer: Yorro Bari, The Gambia, 2013
Dance Artist: Ibrahima Sory Bangoura, Senegal, 2013
Master Dancer: Moundaw Tamba, The Gambia, 2014
Master Drummer: Omar Bunhatap Jammeh, The Gambia, 2013
Historian: Modou Tamba, The Gambia, 2004
Historian: Muhammed Qadir, Morocco, 2010

Books and Articles

Akombo, David. *The Unity of Music and Dance in World Cultures.* Jefferson: McFarland & Company, Inc., 2016.
Atkinson, Quentin D. "Phonemic Diversity Supports A Serial Founder Effect Model of Language Expansion From Africa." *Science* 332, no. 6027 (April 15 2011): 346-49. Accessed July 3, 2019. https://doi.org/10.1126/science.1199295.
Banham, Martin, ed. *A History of Theatre in Africa.* Cambridge: University of Cambridge Press, 2004.
Banham, Martin, Errol Hill and George Woodyard. *The*

Cambridge Guide to African & Caribbean Theatre. Cambridge: Cambridge University Press, 1994.

Baum, Robert M. *Shrines of the Slave Trade: Diola Religion and Society in Precolonial Senegambia.* New York: Oxford University Press, 1999.

Beaman, Patricia. *World Dance Cultures: From Ritual to Spectacle.* London: Routledge, 2018.

Berger, Iris. *South Africa in World History.* Oxford: Oxford University Press, 2009.

Bocquené, Henri. *Mamoirs of a Mbororo; The Life of Ndudi Umaru: Fulani Nomad of Cameroon.* Translated by Philip Burnham and Gordeen Gorder. New York: Bergham Books, 2002.

Bovill, Edward William. *The Golden Trade of the Moors.* Princeton: Markus Wiener Publishers, 2008.

Bowen, T.J. *Adventures and Missionary Labours in Several Countries in the Interior of Africa from 1849 to 1856.* London: Frank Cass & Co., 1857.

Connah, Graham. *African Civilizations: An Archaeological Perspective.* Cambridge: University of Cambridge Press, 2018.

Conneau, Theophilus. *A Slaver's Log Book or 20 Years' Residence in Africa: The Original 1853 Manuscript.* 1853. Reprint, Englewood: Prentice-Hall, Inc., 1976.

Curtis, Matthew C. "Relating the Ancient Ona Culture to the Wider Northern Horn: Discerning Patterns and Problems In the Archaeology of the First Millennium BC." In "Re-evaluating the Archaeology of the First Millennium BC in the Northern Horn," *The African Archaeological Review* 26, no, 4 (December 2009): 327-50. Accessed July 8, 2019. https://jstor.org/stable/40389409.

Dagan, Ester A., ed., *The Spirit's Dance in Africa: Evolution, Transformation and Continuity in Sub-Sahara.* Quebec: Galerie Amrad African Arts Publications, 1997.

De Jong, Ferdinand. *Masquerades of Modernity: Power and Secrecy in Casamance*, Senegal. Bloomington: Indiana University Press, 2007.

Department of the Arts of Africa, Oceania, and the Americas. "The Fulani/Fulbe People." In *Heilbrunn Timeline of Art History*. New York: The Metropolitan Museum of Art, 2000.

Dilley, R.M. *Islamic and Caste Knowledge Practices Among Haalpulaar'en in Senegal: Between Mosque and Termite Mound.* London: Edinburgh University Press, 2004.

Ebron, Paula A. *Performing Africa*. Princeton: Princeton University Press, 2002.

Ehret, Christopher. *The Civilizations of Africa: A History to 1800.* Charlottesville: University of Virginia Press, 2016.

El Hamel, Chouki. *Black Morocco: A History of Slavery, Race, and Islam*. Cambridge: Cambridge University Press, 2015.

Falola, Toyin, ed. *Africa*. Vol. 1, *African History Before 1885*. Durham: Carolina Academic Press, 2000.

Gray, William. *Travels in Western Africa, in the Years 1818, 19, 20, and 21: From the River Gambia, through Wooli, Bodoo, Galam, Kasson, Kaarta, and Foolidoo, to the River Niger.* London: John Murray, Albemarle Street, 1825.

Hamdun, Said and Noel King. *Ibn Battuta in Black Africa*. Princeton: Markus Wiener Publishers, 2010.

Heine, Bernard and Derek Nurse. *African Languages: An Introduction.* Cambridge: Cambridge University Press, 2000.

Heshilwood, Christopher S, Francesco d'Errico, Karen L. van Niekerk, Laure Dayet, Alain Queffelec, and Luca Pollarolo. "An abstract drawing from the 73,000-year-old levels at Blombos Caves, South Africa." *Nature* (2018): 115-18. Accessed July 7, 2019. https://doi.org/10.1038/s41586-018-0514-3.

Huet, Michael. *The Dances of Africa*. Harry N. Abrams, Inc., Publishers, 1994.

_____. *The Dance, Art and Ritual of Africa.* New York: Pantheon Books, 1978.

Kingsley, Mary. *Travels in West Africa.* London: Macmillan, 1897.

Kinney, Lesley. *Dance, Dancers and the Performance Cohort In the Old Kingdom.* 1809. Reprint. Oxford: BAR Publishing, 2016.

Le Quellec, Jean-Löic. *Rock Art in Africa: Mythology and Legend.* Translated by Paul Bahn. Paris: Editions Flammarion, 2004.

Lovejoy, Paul E. *Transformations in Slavery: A History of Slavery in Africa.* Cambridge: Cambridge University Press, 2008.

Levtzion, Nehemia and Jay Spaulding. *Medieval West Africa: Views from Arab Scholars and Merchants.* Princeton: Markus Wiener Publishers, 2007.

Lewis-Williams, David and Sam Challis. *Deciphering Ancient Minds: The Mystery of San Bushman Rock Art.* London: Thames & Hudson, 2011.

Lexova, Irena. *Ancient Egyptian Dances.* Mineola: Dover Publications, Inc., 2000.

McNaughton, Patrick R. *A Bird Dance Near Saturday City: Sidi Ballo and the Art of West African Masquerade.* Bloomington: Indiana University Press, 2008.

Mercader, Julio. "Stone Age Pantry: Archaeologist Unearths Earliest evidence of Modern Humans Using Wild Grains and Tubers for Food." *Science* 326, no. 5960 (December 18, 2009). Accessed June 21, 2019. www.sciencedaily.com/releases/2009/12/091217141312.htm.

Miers, Suzanne and Igor Kopytoff, editors. *Slavery in Africa: Historical and Anthropological Perspectives.* Madison: University of Wisconsin Press, 1979.

Moktar, G., ed. *General History of Africa.* Vol. 2. *Ancient*

Civilizations of Africa. Berkeley: University of California Press, 1990.

Nii-Yartey, Francis. *African Dance in Ghana: Contemporary Transformations*. London: Mot Juste Limited, 2012.

Nzongola-Ntalaja, Georges. *The Congo from Leopold to Kabila: A People's History*. London: Zed Books, 2007.

Park, Mungo. *Travels in the Interior Districts of Africa: Performed Under the Direction and Patronage of the African Association in the Years 1795, 1796, and 1797*. London: W. Bulmer and Co., 1799.

Pellizi, Francesco. *Res 59/60: Anthropology and Aesthetics* (Spring/Autumn, 2011) New York: The Peabody Museum of Archaeology and Ethnology and the Harvard University Art Museums.

Plastow, Jane. "Ethiopia and Eritrea." In *A History of Theatre In Africa*, edited by Martin Banham, 192-205. Cambridge: Cambridge University Press, 2004.

Reed, Daniel B. *Dan Ge Performance: Masks and Music in Contemporary Côte d'Ivoire*. Bloomington: Indiana University Press, 2003.

Segal, Ronald. *Islam's Black Slaves: The Other Black Diaspora*. New York: Farrar, Straus and Giroux, 2001.

Shaw, Thomas M. *The Fulani Matrix of Beauty and Art in the Djolof Region of Senegal*. Lewiston: The Edwin Mellen Press, 1994.

Shillington, Kevin. *History of Africa*. London: Palgrave Macmillan, 2012.

Sonko-Godwin, Patience. *Ethnic Groups of The Senegambia Region: A Brief History*. Banjul, The Gambia: Sunrise Publishers, 2003.

Spencer, Paul, editor. *Society and the Dance: The Social Anthropology of Process and Performance*. London: Cambridge University Press, 2003.

Sullivan, Sian and Chris Low. "Shades of the Rainbow Serpent?

A KhoeSan Animal Between Myth and Landscape in Southern Africa – Ethnographic Contextualisations of Rock Art Representations." *Arts* 3 (2014). Accessed July 6, 2019. https://doi.org/10.3390/arts302015.

Tamari, Tal. "The Development of Caste Systems in West Africa." *The Journal of African History* 32, no. 2 (1991). Accessed September 24, 2012. https://www.jstore.org/stable/182616.

Tierou, Alphonse. *Doople: The Eternal Law of African Dance*. New York: Routledge, 1989.

Tracey, Andrew. "The Nyanga Panpipe Dance." *African Music: Journal of the International Library of African Music* 5, no. 1 (July 1971): 73-89. Accessed April 30, 2019. https://doi.org/10.21504/amj.v5i1.1152

Vogt, Yngve. Translated by Alan Lewis Belardinelli. "World's Oldest Ritual Discovered. Worshipped the Python 70,000 Years Ago." *Apollon Research Magazine*. University of Oslo (February 1, 2012). Accessed July 6, 2019. https://www.apollon.uio.no/english/articles/2006/python-english.html.

Weil, Peter M. "Women's Masks and the Power of Gender in Mande History." *African Arts* 31, no. 2. Special Issue. "Women's Masquerades in Africa and the Diaspora" (Spring, 1998): 28-37+88+90+94-95. Accessed July 7, 2012. https://www.jstor.org/stable/3337517.

Wells, Spencer. *The Journey of Man: A Genetic Odyssey*. Princeton: Princeton University Press, 2017.

Wright, John. *The Trans-Saharan Slave Trade*. London: Routledge, 2010.

Zarrilli, Phillip B. et al. Editors. *Theatre Histories: An Introduction*. 2nd ed. New York: Routledge, 2010.

DVD/Video

Bangoura, Moustapha. *Tinkanyi 1*. DVD. Produced by Marc Sandrolini of Quietcity Productions, 2004.
Bangoura, Moustapha. *Tinkanyi 2*. DVD. Produced by Marc Sandrolini of Quietcity Productions, 2004.
Bangoura, Moustapha. *Tinkanyi 3*. DVD. Produced by Le Bagatae, 2016.
Bangoura, Moustapha. *Tinkanyi 4*. DVD. Produced by Le Bagatae, 2016.
Koumbassa, Youssouf. *Let's Go Wangai 1: Dances from Guinea West Africa*. DVD. B-rave Studio Production, 1999.
Koumbassa, Youssouf. *Let's Go Wangai 2: Dances from Guinea West Africa*. DVD. B-rave Studio Production, 1999.
Les Ballets Africains, The National Dance Company of the Republic of Guinea. *Jubilee*. DVD. World Music Productions, Inc., 2004.
Les Ballets Africains, The National Dance Company of the Republic of Guinea. *Memoire du Manding*. DVD. Large Scale Productions, LLC and World Arts Inc., 2007.
Les Ballets Bagata in Concert. Kooyinma, directed by Youssouff Kombassa. DVD. B-rave Studio, 1996.

Index

Africa 11-5, 17, 21-5, 28, 30, 32 37, 43-4, 46, 49, 55, 57, 63, 72-3, 79, 80, 82, 87, 89, 90, 93, 99, 100: Northern 37: Eastern 55: Western 72: Central 88-90, 93
Africanized Islam 49
Ajamat 75-6, 78
Aksum 57, 59

BaNtu 23-5, 30, 32, 63, 93
bells 67
Blombos Cave 28
Burundi 15, 63, 65-6
Bushing 95

Chad 13, 16, 87, 89-91: Lake 13, 16, 90
Congo 15, 65, 87, 93, 95, 100: Democratic Republic of 15, 63, 87, 93, 95, 100
contractions 9, 61, 91: torso 9, 61, 91: pelvic 9, 91
cowrie shells 43, 50, 78, 95, 98
culture xi-xiii, 3-5, 7, 10, 15, 25, 26, 37, 44, 47, 49, 55, 57, 66, 73, 90, 100,

Dance xi-ii, 1, 4, 5, 7-9, 11, 13, 21, 23, 25-6, 28, 29, 31, 32, 34, 39-41, 43-4, 49, 51, 57, 60-1, 66-8, 71, 76, 81, 83, 91, 97, 100: history xii-iii, 4, 21, 71: phrase 9, 34, 49: systems xiii, 3-4, 10, 39, 44, 59, 76, 100: step 9, 11, 34, 67, 76, 81, 83, 97, 100
dennaboo 81
dynasty 40, 59, 65, 96

Egypt 37, 39-41, 43
Eskista 60-1, 63
Ethiopia 15, 55, 57, 59, 61
ethnic groups xii, 23-4, 60, 63, 66, 75, 79, 84, 90, 93, 95

Fula Fare 81
Fulani 47, 79-81, 83-4

Gambia, The 44, 73, 75, 78, 100
gangué 91
Gnawa 44, 47, 49-51
Hutu 63
Instrument 32, 49-50, 62, 78

Intore 66-8
ITCZ 15

Jola 76

Kasa 75-6, 78
Khoikhoi 21, 23
Kiantapo 87
kingdom 39-40, 44, 46, 63, 66, 93: old 40: middle 40: new 39, 43
Klag 90-2
krakeb 48-9, 51
Kuba 95, 97: cloth 98
!Kung 23, 26, 28
kutiro 78
kuyu 51

Lalibela 59
lila 51

Mbaye 90, 92
Mbororo 79-80, 83
migration 7, 15, 21, 25, 71, 95
monoliths 73, 75, 100
Morocco 14, 44, 46-7, 50
movement vocabulary 9, 31, 41, 49, 51, 61, 67, 68, 81, 91, 97
Mozambique 23, 30, 32
muqadma 51
Muu 41, 43
Mwaash Mbooy 95, 97

Niger-Congo 24-5, 79
Nilo-Saharan 24
Nubia xii, 37, 39

Nyanga 32, 34
Nyungwe 30, 32
Pulaku 80

qemis 61-2

raffia 30, 67, 78, 91, 95, 97
Ramesseum 43
religious 7, 39, 41, 43-4, 47, 51, 59, 60, 75, 84, 95
rite of passage 43, 80
rock art xii, 28, 80: church 59: paintings 13, 80: engravings 100
royal dance 66, 68

sacred 61: dance 47, 51: ceremonies 49, 61
Sahara 13: Desert 16-7, 37, 65
San 21, 23-5, 28-30
Senegal 25, 44, 71, 73, 75, 79, 100: River 73
Senegambia 44, 46, 75
Southern Africa 14, 21, 23, 25, 28, 32
Sub-Saharan 37, 44, 46-7, 90
tam tam 91-2
torso 9, 51, 61-2, 67, 78, 90, 97: acute 78, 83, 90
tribe 8
Tutsi: 23, 63, 66-8
trans-Saharan 47, 49-50, 90

Yoleli 81, 83

Zagwe 59

www.ingramcontent.com/pod-product-compliance
Lightning Source LLC
Chambersburg PA
CBHW061221070526
44584CB00029B/3924